SON OF THE PASSION

Son of the Passion

The Story of
Gabriel Francis Possenti
the New Patron of Catholic Youth
for the Universal Church

by

Godfrey Poage, C.P.

The Bruce Publishing Company • *Milwaukee*

NIHIL OBSTAT:

    FREDERICK SUCHER, C.P., S.T.D.
    Censor for the Congregation of the Passion

IMPRIMI POTEST:

    WALTER KAELIN, C.P.
    Provincial of Holy Cross Province
    February 27, 1962

NIHIL OBSTAT:

    JOHN F. MURPHY, S.T.D.
    Censor librorum

IMPRIMATUR:

    ✠ WILLIAM E. COUSINS
    Archbishop of Milwaukee
    April 13, 1962

Library of Congress Catalog Card Number: 62–16840

© 1962 THE BRUCE PUBLISHING COMPANY
MADE IN THE UNITED STATES OF AMERICA

INTRODUCTION

"As in former ages God raised up Stanislaus and Aloysius as models for Christian youth, so in this twentieth century He has given us this son of Umbria, Gabriel Francis Possenti. We, therefore, name him the new patron of youth for the Universal Church. . . ."*

Thus on May 21, 1920, His Holiness, Pope Benedict XV, directed the attention of the whole Catholic world to the example of Gabriel of the Sorrowful Virgin. "What this Passionist student achieved in less than six years of religious life," the pontiff pointed out, "is a lesson and an inspiration to everyone."

The Holy Father's choice aroused great interest in Europe. Italians were especially enthusiastic and Isola Gran Sasso, a remote mountain village in east-central Italy, became such a favorite place of pilgrims that the government built a special highway over the mountains to accommodate them.

But little notice was given this new patron in the United States. Few Americans even heard about Gabriel Francis Possenti and the Passionist Congregation of which he was so distinguished a member.

One reason for this ignorance and neglect was the lack of publicity. Very little appeared in English about him,

---

* *Acta Apos. Sedis*, Vol. XII, May, 1920.

and what was written was little more than a commentary
on the Passionist way of life. His real story was never told.

Over forty years have passed since the Holy Father
picked Gabriel Possenti as the special patron for twentieth-
century youth. On February 27, 1962, we celebrated the
centenary of his death. This book, therefore, is long
overdue.

In preparing the biography, microfilms were made of
the complete processes of canonization: three thousand,
six hundred and ninety-two pages of sworn testimony given
by relatives and associates of the saint before various
papal commissions. From such material a chronology was
evolved, covering every month of Gabriel's life and re-
quiring over six hundred manuscript pages. Finally, all the
places mentioned in the book were visited and available
material there studied. "On-the-spot" descriptions were
made with a portable dictaphone and over a thousand
photographs taken.

In the final editing this extensive research was sum-
marized. In several places it was necessary to enliven the
account with dialogue, but where this was done every
word was first checked against the sworn testimony of witnesses in the processes. Nothing was said that had not been
quoted by eyewitnesses, at least in the third person. Lastly,
those who participated in the research were given manuscript copies of the book to compare with the *Life of
Francis Possenti* by his contemporary, Father Paul Bonaccia, and the manuscript of the "Life of Confrater Gabriel
of the Sorrowful Virgin," by his director, Father Norbert
Cassinelli of Holy Mary. This latter document was found in
the provincial archives of the Passionist monastery at
Recanati during the course of the research.

The present book has been five years in preparation and represents the combined efforts of many individuals. Particular gratitude is due Brother John Joseph Stearns, C.F.X., and Father Vincent Mary Oberhauser, C.P., for help in the preliminary research; to Fathers Roger Mercurio, C.P., and Columban Browning, C.P., for translations; and to Mr. Francis McGrade for editorial suggestions.

FATHER GODFREY POAGE, C.P.
Retreat of the Immaculate Conception
Chicago, Illinois

Feast of St. Gabriel of the Sorrowful Virgin,
February 27, 1962

CONTENTS

SON OF THE PASSION

CHAPTER I

STONES FOR BREAD

*"If one of you asks his father for bread,
will he hand him a stone?"*   (Lk. 11:10.)

Rumors of cholera reached Spoleto in north-central Italy around the end of May, 1855. The news struck terror into every heart. Once before in 1848–1849 this dread disease had struck Europe, killing hundreds of thousands of people across the continent. Spoleto had been spared in the earlier epidemic, but now cholera was at its doorstep, and at the beginning of June it struck and spread with terrifying speed, visiting every street and entering nearly every home.

In the Possenti household it was Maria Louise who was stricken. Ever since their mother had died, in 1842, she and the father, Sante, had kept up the home. With eleven brothers and sisters she had had plenty to keep her busy.

Pacifica, the family's devoted governess, put Maria Louise to bed and sent her brother, Francis, running after Doctor Mariani. He found the exhausted physician almost beside himself. There were so many calls, he had scarcely time to eat. But he promised to come as soon as possible.

1

Francis returned to the sickroom and stood at the bedside of his stricken sister. Her face was now taking on a grayish hue and her long hair was drenched with sweat. As he tried to fan her she smiled weakly in appreciation.

Francis had heard about this horrible malady and how it compressed an infinity of suffering within the few days of its fearful course. First came the cold, clammy sweat; then the skin shrank and grew dark gray. Next came cramps of violent intensity in the calves of the legs and in the arms. Added to this was an unquenchable thirst. Finally, just before death, the circulation grew so sluggish that even cutting the veins would fail to produce a flow of blood. Maria Louise was already in the first stage of this disease, and if it could not be checked, there was little hope for her life.

An hour went by . . . and then another. Noon came. The sun was high and hot and not a breadth of air stirred in the sickroom. The doctor had not come. Francis went to the window and looked anxiously up and down the street. Everybody seemed to be indoors, as though afraid to meet the cholera abroad.

He decided to try again to get medical help. "I'll be back in a little while," he said, looking down in Maria Louise's dark, deep-circled eyes and trying to smile. Then he hastily left the room, closing the door carefully behind him.

There was a municipal hospital just half a mile away, and Francis hoped that if he couldn't get the family doctor, one of the others would come. The sun seemed to scorch him, as he ran down the Via Loreto, and his temples began to throb from the heat. As he neared the hospital he heard the babble of many voices. Turning into the courtyard, he found the place seething with activity. It was like an overturned anthill. People were running in and out of the building, panic in their faces. On the steps little children sat crying unattended. There were wagons and coaches, crowded with pale and sickly people, their drivers cursing to get through the crowds.

After working his way across the threshold, Francis stopped appalled. Lying in rows were hundreds of men, women, and children. Some lay stiff and still, but many were writhing in pain and moaning. Everywhere swarms of flies hovered over the helpless victims or crawled across their faces. The smell of sweat, of unwashed bodies, of human excrement, rose up in the waves of suffocating heat. The stench almost nauseated him. Nurses and doctors were hurrying here and there among the prostrate forms, sometimes bumping an arm or leg, so thickly packed were the rows. The victims scarcely bothered to complain, staring stonily up, waiting their turn.

At the end of the hall he saw Doctor Mariani. As he picked his way through the stricken bodies, feverish hands plucked at his trousers and voices croaked for water.

Cold little ripples of fear started in the pit of his stomach and radiated outward until his arms and legs trembled. Gingerly he stepped over a dead man who lay dull-eyed with hands clutching his stomach.

At length he reached the doctor, who was coatless and whose sleeves were rolled up to his shoulders. His face was that of a man drunk with fatigue. It was gray and dusty, and sweat had streaked long rivulets across his cheeks. Seeing Francis, he exclaimed: "Thank God, you are here. I can use every pair of hands."

For a moment Francis stared at him in bewilderment.

"Come here, boy, lift this patient's head!"

"But, Doctor," Francis stammered, "I want you to come over to our house to help Maria Louise. She's got the cholera!"

"Great God!" thundered the doctor and his face was suddenly contorted with rage. "Are you crazy? I can't leave these people. They are dying, hundreds of them. I can't leave them for your sister or anybody else!"

Francis began to shake and his eyes burned with tears of fright. The doctor wasn't coming with him. Maria Louise would die. The doctor refused to help.

"In the name of God, Doctor! Please!"

Doctor Mariani bit his lip, but his anger cooled. "Son, I'll try. I can't promise you. But I'll try. When we get these patients tended to . . ."

Immediately he turned to a nurse and began pointing to various victims. Blindly, Francis worked his way out of the hospital and ran home. His father, his brother Vincent, and Pacifica were waiting anxiously in the sickroom. As they looked to him for word of the doctor, he was panting so hard from his running that words would not come. He just shook his head and looked pityingly at his prostrate sister.

Late that evening Doctor Mariani stopped by to check on the patient. "There is not much I can do," he said, "except leave some sedatives and salt tablets. More than a thousand people are trying to get help at the hospital and I wouldn't be surprised if half the town is stricken before this plague is over. The only thing that can stop it is prayer!"

For days Maria Louise lingered between life and death. Sometimes the medicine seemed to take effect, but then there would be a relapse. As he looked at his sister's pain-wasted face, Francis couldn't help wondering why she, of all people in the world, should be so afflicted. It seemed that Maria Louise had always taken care of him and his brothers and sisters. It had been Maria Louise to whom he had so often run as a child, when he was hurt or frightened. It had been her tender kisses that dried his tears, and her quiet voice that drove away his fears. Now she was dying and he could do nothing to help her.

As the Feast of Corpus Christi approached, on June 7, he remembered that he had been appointed to be cross-bearer for the procession at the cathedral. At first he didn't want to leave his sister, but his father reassured him. "I know she would want you to go . . . and I doubt if there will be any change in her condition."

Francis took his hat and went out into the silent streets. As he trudged up the back lane to the cathedral, his mind was still in the sickroom, his heart heavy with grief. Almost mechanically he went into the sacristy and put on his cassock and surplice.

As the procession moved slowly out of the cathedral to the first altar in the piazza, the words of the *Pange Lingua* touched the depths of his soul, filling him with a wild hope that his prayers would be answered and his sister would be snatched from the grave.

Suddenly Vincent came up behind him and tugged gently at the sleeve of his surplice. He turned his head slightly. Breathlessly his brother whispered, "Come home as quickly as you can. Maria Louise is dead."

Francis went through the rest of the ceremony in a daze. As soon as the third Benediction was concluded, he pulled off his surplice and cassock and ran the five blocks home. The violent exertion stirred his body, but his mind seemed to be in a world he had never known before. Even familiar objects looked different.

When he entered the sickroom and looked upon the sightless eyes of his second mother, something strange and indescribable took place within his soul. The corpse of his twenty-six-year-old sister was turning rigid and cold. The remark of his former spiritual director, Father Tedeschini, came to his mind: "All things in this world are but vanities, deceits, and frivolities." In that hour of pain and anguish he grew to manhood. His sister's death more than anything else made him realize the purpose of man's life upon earth.

Maria Louise was buried in the cemetery east of town, for the municipal government had forbidden the use of family burial vaults for cholera victims. It was a sad little procession that followed her body down the cypress-lined road and into the plot Sante Possenti had purchased. The pallbearers, classmates of Francis from the Jesuit college, set the coffin down near the grave and stood clenching and unclenching their aching fingers. Sante, Pacifica, Vincent, and Francis — now the only ones still living at home — filed in behind the priest and servers. A few friends of the family brought up the rear.

Dully Francis listened to the prayers of Father Joseph Piccone and watched the blessing of the grave. Then taking a small trowel the priest sprinkled a few grains of dirt over the coffin and passed the trowel to the family. As Francis, in turn, threw a little dust into the grave of his sister, it seemed that he was also casting into the ground the remnants of his gay and irresponsible youth.

For the next six weeks the plague seemed to increase in intensity. The town became like a morgue, and only the most necessary activities were carried on. There were no amusements. The Opera House was closed. Families who were on the best of terms ceased to visit each other. With death so close at hand, no one dared think of pleasure. An air of gloom and despondency settled upon the city.

In the Possenti home there was deeper gloom. The loss of Maria Louise was like a culminating sorrow to the already heavy burden that Sante had borne for years. It seemed to leave him a broken man, and he now clung all the more tenaciously to the two sons who remained at home, Francis and Vincent.

The epidemic reached its height around the middle of August, 1855, and the terror-stricken people hardly knew where to turn. Then faith asserted itself and word sped through the town: "The icon will save us!"

Frantically the able-bodied people in town thronged to the great square in front of the *Duomo,* pleading with the archbishop to bless them with an image of the Madonna which was preserved in the cathedral. This famous Byzantine picture was the patronal Madonna of Spoleto and tradition claimed it had been painted by St. Luke. Its colors had faded through the years, but the face of the Virgin Mother was soft and sad. The eyes seemed partly closed.

Originally the icon belonged to the patriarchal church of Constantinople, but it had been brought to Rome in the eighth century to save it from the fury of the Iconoclasts, who felt that all religious images were superstitious.

In 1115 the Emperor Frederick Barbarossa gave it to the city of Spoleto to conciliate the people after his armies had raped their women and ravaged their countryside.

The picture was also of great monetary value. The entire surface, except the head and shoulders of the Madonna, was overlaid in gold. The crown was studded with diamonds, rubies, and emeralds, while the frame itself was encircled with matched pearls. The city had accepted this treasure as a sign of peace and reconciliation, and from that day on the Mother of God had secured for the Spoletans many divine favors. Now they felt that if anything could save them it would be their icon.

Archbishop Arnaldi agreed to the pleas of the crowd and in the name of the whole diocese vowed a public procession each year on the octave day of Mary's Feast of the Assumption, if only she would spare them. He then brought the icon to the steps of the cathedral and blessed the afflicted city.

Almost immediately, it seemed, Mary heard their supplications. From that moment on no more deaths occurred, nor were any new cases of cholera reported. After a few days almost every trace of the epidemic disappeared. The city cast off its signs of grief and rejoiced in the happiness of being delivered so speedily from the plague. A solemn procession of thanksgiving was held, and life at Spoleto began to slip back into its old routine.

There was a change, though, in Francis Possenti. He was becoming increasingly quiet and reserved, and everyone noticed how he was spending more and more time in his room before his little shrine of the Pieta. He wanted Mary to enlighten him in regard to his vocation. Years earlier he had promised to become a priest. But what kind?

The Passionists were certainly the most popular missionaries in the area and their life appealed strongly to him. Yet what should he do if his father objected?

Sante Possenti was now sixty-six years old and, though he held the high position of assessor at the supreme court in Spoleto, it was time for him to retire. God had blessed him with a goodly portion of this world's goods, but so much was now slipping away. Of his thirteen children, seven had already been claimed by death, together with his wife, Agnes. Of the six still living, Louis was a Dominican priest and Henry was studying at the diocesan seminary. Teresa was married and Michael was away at medical school. Francis and Vincent, with their governess Pacifica, were the only ones living at home.

It was natural, therefore, for Sante to turn more and more to these two boys. He needed them for companionship and support in his declining years. Of the two, it was quite obvious that Francis' talents and personality singled him out as the one best able to maintain their fortune and carry on the Possenti name. Moreover, in many of their talks together Sante had told Francis of his confidence in the boy and how he relied especially on him to be his father's comfort and support.

Francis, for his part, had other plans. He knew it would be a keen disappointment to his father to learn that he had decided to leave the world and relinquish all the bright prospects of success it promised. Still, difficult as it was, some announcement had to be made. The sooner Sante found out, the better it would be.

Accordingly, summoning up his courage and invoking the help of his heavenly Mother, Francis went down to his father's study one evening, as the old man sat reading.

The door was ajar, so he entered without knocking. Sante looked up with a pleased smile, and Francis closed the door.

Francis wished at the moment that his heart would beat more slowly. He had planned this meeting very carefully and wanted to remember exactly what he had decided to tell his father . . . but his thoughts were jumbled.

"Why all the secrecy, son?" Sante asked. Francis gulped. How kind his father looked, sitting there with his dark, twinkling eyes and white hair, all unaware of his son's excitement.

Francis stepped across the room and took a chair in front of his father. A thousand incoherent thoughts shot through his mind, but he could not catch hold of a single one to mold it into words.

"What is it," Sante asked. "A secret to tell me?"

Suddenly Francis found his tongue and just as suddenly all his finely reasoned explanations fell away. He blurted out, "Yes — a secret. I want to become a Passionist."

For an instant there was a silence so acute it seemed that neither of them even breathed. Then the trembling fell away from Francis, as happiness and pride surged through him. Why hadn't he done this before? How much simpler than all the timid maneuverings he had planned. Then his eyes sought those of his father.

There was a look of consternation in them. It was almost the look he had seen the day they had received the news that his brother Paul had been shot by the Austrian soldiers in a student uprising at the University of Venice. Or worse still, the shock that his father had when he learned that his oldest son Lawrence had been identified by the police as a member of the *Carbonari* and had apparently committed suicide. But then the old man laughed.

"Now I've heard everything! What won't you think of next? You — my Checchino!" he exclaimed, using the familiar nickname the family had given Francis. "Of all things . . . a Passionist! I can just see you in a monastery . . . you, who up till now have thought of nothing save a good time. You like to dress in the latest styles . . . to go to the theater . . . to hunt and ride. Ha! You'd make a great religious!"

"But I'm serious, Father!" Francis stammered, and unbidden tears flooded his eyes.

Suddenly the mask on Sante's face was gone. "You mustn't make such wild statements, Checchino! You don't mean them. You'll make yourself the laughingstock of the town, and you'll be ashamed later for telling me!"

A hot swift current of anger and determination was running through Francis and he snapped back: "I've never been more serious in all my life! I mean it! And I'm going through with it!"

Suddenly he stopped. Never had he seen such misery on anyone's face. "Father, you will grant me permission . . . won't you? Let me at least try."

"I suppose there is nothing else I can do," Sante answered dully. "But I'll have to have time to think it over."

If Sante had disowned him, Francis could not have been more frightened. He looked at his father pleadingly. "What do you mean by that?"

"I want you to take at least a year," Sante said, regaining some of his old magisterial air. "I want you to mix in society and forget all the tragedies that have come to our family. I want you to know life that is beautiful and attractive. I want you to go to dances and balls, attend the opera, and enjoy yourself. Then after a year, if you still want to be a Passionist I will think about giving my consent. After all, you still have another year of school, and it would be senseless to rush off without your college degree. You do as I say for a year, then I may reconsider. But until that time, not another word to me about the Passionists!"

Filial love and respect conquered what little rebellion Francis had felt for a moment. "All right, Papa," he murmured, and getting up he walked slowly out of the room.

CHAPTER II

LOVE NOT THE WORLD

> *"Young men . . . do not love the world,*
> *or the things that are in the world . . .*
> *because all that is in the world is the lust*
> *of the flesh, and the lust of the eyes, and*
> *the pride of life."* (1 Jn. 2:14, 15.)

In November Francis Possenti began his senior year at the Jesuit college on the Via Cerquiglia, and within a very short time he was back into the old routine. True to his promise he threw himself once more into the social and academic life of the town. He had fun, more fun than he had ever had before. Spoleto was trying to make up for its sorrows, and it had become a boisterous, exciting place.

The Pannechetti family was one of the first to have a party and they naturally invited Sante and his two sons because the Possentis were their close friends. Judge Pannechetti was chief justice of the Spoleto supreme court and the acknowledged social leader. For the occasion Francis got a new linen shirt, trimmed with dainty embroidery and infinitesimal tucks, together with a wide silk cravat. Both were in the latest fashion and went well with his fawn-colored trousers and dark blue coat.

Francis felt a rising excitement as he looked over the merry throng that gathered that evening for the ball. The whole house was ablaze with candlelight, and down each side of the room ran flower-decked tables heaped high with food and drink. Long graceful ropes of ivy and smilax draped over the windows and twined in scallops along the walls. At the end of the room was a raised platform for the musicians, but it was almost hidden from view by banked greenery and bright red bunting.

Happy excitement was the mood of the early evening, and Francis found himself bowing and greeting the guests as they arrived and congratulating one another simply for being alive. There were so many girls, it seemed to him, girls he had hardly noticed before. Now they looked beautiful in butterfly bright dresses which were hooped out enormously. Lace shawls hung carelessly from their arms, and fans of swan's-down and peacock feathers dangled from ribbons at their wrists. Some of the girls had their hair smoothed sleekly back from their ears into chignons, so heavy that their heads seemed tilted back in saucy pride. Others had masses of curls about their necks and fringed gold earbobs that tossed and danced with every playful gesture. Laces, silks, ribbons and all the finery of Spoleto seemed assembled in the room that night.

There were several uniforms in the crowd, too, for Judge Pannechetti had invited the officers of *La Rocca*, the old fortress that commanded the approach to Spoleto. The soldiers were splendidly outfitted with shining buttons and dazzling gold epaulets entwined with braid. Red and yellow stripes set off the blue of their uniforms. Scarlet and gold sashes swung to and fro, sabers glittered and slapped against shining boots.

Francis felt a swell of pride in his heart as he acknowl-edged greetings, waved to friends, and bent low over the hands of ladies. The hubbub of voices made it almost impossible to hear individual remarks. Finally, the orches-tra struck up *Parla Mi D'Amore*. It was time for the first dance.

Francis looked across the room at Maria Pannechetti. He had known her from childhood and observed that she was now quite an attractive young lady with almond eyes and dark complexion. Her rose organdy dress with a long pink sash set off these charms, and her gown billowed over the hoops and matched her red morocco slippers.

Crossing the room Francis took her hand and claimed the first dance. Her mother beamed approval, her thoughts soaring far beyond the party to a possible future union of the Possenti and Pannechetti families.

If Francis had known of her aspirations, he would only have laughed. He liked all the girls and danced with as many as he could. His companions, quick to notice this trait, nicknamed him *Il Ballerino* — "the dancer." Francis' many friends also enjoyed his ability to clown and to make them laugh.

They also called him *Il Damerino* — "the dude," prob-ably a reference to his immaculate grooming, because he was hardly good-looking. From his father he inherited a broad forehead and abundant dark hair. His large, frank eyes and rather small mouth came from his mother. From her he also received his aquiline features and rounded chin. His ears stuck out too prominently — almost like jug handles.

But more important than these physical endowments were the moral traits that were obvious to his boyhood acquaintances. He had much of his father's courage and determination, with a straightforwardness and complete honesty of purpose. He also had his mother's independence of thought and action, and he could at times be stubborn.

Francis always liked to think things out for himself. Once he made up his mind to do something, it was difficult to induce him to change. He did not put up with opposition easily, and sometimes, when thwarted in his desires he would stamp his feet in uncontrolled anger and his face would flush. In one such mood he struck his brother Henry, who was three years older and quite capable of defending himself against Francis. Henry lashed back and Francis turned to run. His brother tried to stop him and slammed the door. It caught Francis on the nose and knocked him down. The blow broke his nose, but no one realized this until the next morning. It was then too late to do much about setting the bone. Ever afterward his nose was slightly crooked. Francis used to joke about it and say it proved his courage.

In the fall, when the great opera companies from Rome and Milan presented their repertoire, he could be found in his father's box almost every night. The brilliant stage, the stirring music, and the dramatic action fascinated him. Two of the operas he enjoyed were the sensationally tuneful and dramatic *Il Trovatore* by Joseph Verdi, and Mozart's *Don Giovanni*. Francis learned the lyrics of both operas and delighted in singing them for his friends.

Sante was pleased to see his son enjoying life. He figured it would be only a matter of time before Francis forgot his foolish dreams of the monastery. But occasionally he would wonder . . . like the night Francis became bored with a poor performance and slipped out of the Opera House during intermission. Sante had followed him and found him walking up and down the piazza in front of the cathedral saying his beads.

At college Francis maintained excellent grades. He never won any recognition in mathematics or science, but he more than compensated for this in philosophy and literature. He was proficient in Greek and Latin and could read and write both fluently. Almost effortlessly he tossed off epigrams and odes, both profound and humorous. One of his poems was titled "Death Hidden in the Garments of the Doctor," and another was an ode to "A Fly That Falls in the Milk."

Religious topics, however, seem to have been his favorites, and he wrote a long Latin poem on the "Maternity of Mary" and another in Italian on "Mary's Sorrows." Both subjects became more and more his inspiration in the years ahead.

The thought of death and eternity also captivated him. In his "Ode to a Sun Dial" he asked, "Will the present hour, so quickly slipping by, be, perhaps, the one in which I'll die?" He then concludes on a somber note: "Not all that glitters in the morning shines at night!"

He belonged to a loose-knit association of his classmates, called the "Lords of Spoleto," and often after school hours, like student groups everywhere, they delighted in marching through the streets, laughing and joking and playing tricks on one another. One of their most boisterous stunts was to race their horses through town and rear the mounts to see if the horses could pound some unsuspecting householder's door with their hooves. When the group cut up like this, the police generally looked the other way, for the members included youths from some of the most prominent families.

One thing that embarrassed Francis with this gang of his was the fact that his father had bought him a very fashionable silk top hat and insisted on his wearing it, even to school. His friends thought the hat was slightly ridiculous and they teased him about it constantly. Francis got his revenge by drawing caricatures of them in even more ludicrous hats.

As is inevitable with such groups, the "Lords of Spoleto" had to prove their maturity by smoking. Michael one day caught Francis puffing on one of their father's cigars, and told him to stop.

Jauntily Francis flipped the cigar out the window. But from then on he smoked in secret. He knew that neither his father nor Pacifica would approve, so he never smoked in front of them — only with his companions in the back streets of Spoleto. Then he would carefully air out his jacket, so the scent could not be detected.

One of the youths who became a very close friend of Francis was Philip Giovannetti. The incident that brought them together occurred one morning in the rhetoric class at the Jesuit college. The professor, Father Incelli, S.J., was late and the students began scuffling with one another. It was the "Lords of Spoleto" against the others. Pieces of chalk began flying back and forth across the room, and a regular melee broke out.

"Come on, Philip," one of Francis' group called, "you're on our side!"

"I'm not on anybody's side right now. We're supposed to be studying."

"You'll fight, if I say so," one of the boys told him in bullying tones.

"No! I won't! And you can't make me!"

The boy slapped Philip contemptuously across the face, but Philip took it quietly, and in a perfectly calm voice he answered, "I hope you are satisfied. I forgive you. Now leave me alone."

The assailant withdrew, feeling like a fool. Francis stepped up and offered Philip an apology for the conduct of his associate. From that moment each had a new respect for the other and a fondness that only increased with the years, and from then on they spent a great deal of time together. They liked to play chess and cards, often making small side bets on the games. Both of them believed it made for more excitement in their playing.

One of the projects on which they worked several weeks was a Christmas crib with moving figurines. Francis did the carving and Philip did the painting. A geared device enabled the angels to be moved up and down; Mary to bend low in adoration over the Infant, and Joseph to move back and forth in a protecting way. At Christmas time they displayed it in the Giovannetti home, with Francis manipulating the figures.

On some weekends Francis and Philip took hikes down the valley of the Tessino. Francis showed his companion his favorite spots for snares and traps, and demonstrated his bird calls. He could whistle and trill so cleverly that the birds themselves were fooled and would come flying to him. Once he caught and tamed a screech owl, although he never could imitate its scream. He also trained some homing pigeons and the two friends used them to send notes to one another.

Another friend of a very different kind was Major O'Reilly, the newly appointed commandant at the papal fortress of *La Rocca*. This soldier of fortune had left Ireland in the uprising of 1849, spent some four years in training papal troops, and then obtained a commission from Cardinal Antonnelli.

Major O'Reilly was a capable soldier. He knew how to handle a gun and was well versed in the care and training of cavalry horses. The papal army needed men of his caliber, so Cardinal Antonnelli, the secretary of state under Pope Pius IX, never questioned his background. He accepted the major for what he was, an honest and capable soldier, and gave him command of the garrison at Spoleto. Almost two hundred troops were quartered there, and it was his duty to keep them in fighting trim.

O'Reilly liked Spoleto and came to be accepted by the elite of the town. One of the things that helped him socially was his friendship with the Possentis. He took a fancy to Francis and taught him the fine points of riding, showed him how to care for a gun, and let him practice on the rifle range. Francis became so proficient with a firearm that before long he could pick off a bird on the wing.

Sante was pleased with this new interest and for Christmas that year gave Francis a shotgun. From then on Checchino practically lived outdoors. Some weeks he went almost daily after school across the aqueduct of Ponte delle Tori and climbed Monte Luco, a great hill that rises some three thousand feet just east of Spoleto. Its slopes were densely covered with chestnut trees and ilex oaks, which made good cover for hunting.

One day on the mountain he happened to meet a hermit

by the name of Spada, an old man who had wandered over from nearby Cesi, found an abandoned cave near the summit of Monte Luco, and made it his hermitage. The cave was believed to have once been used by St. Bernardine of Siena.

Francis hadn't known about this newcomer, and he was quite startled when he met him. It was almost like an apparition. Spada, who was then at least seventy years old, was ragged and unkempt. His cheeks were leathery and bristled with whiskers. His large gray eyes peered out from under matted eyebrows, and his whole face seemed framed in an aura of snow-white hair.

Spada showed Francis his little cell partly concealed behind a jutting rock. It was about eight feet deep and ten feet wide and just high enough for a man to stand. Against the back wall was a reed mat, where the old man slept, and in the corner a box on which lay a Bible and a well-worn meditation book with a rosary. His food, he explained, was stored inside the box.

Francis was fascinated by what he saw, and everything about the hermit stirred his curiosity. He wondered what makes a man withdraw from society — and why does he practice such penance.

Old Spada gave him an explanation of the hermitical life and told the boy that he was simply trying to do what St. Paul did. "I want to chastise my body and bring it under subjection. I want to feel in my flesh some of the pains of our Crucified Savior."

As the old man continued his explanations, Francis' awe turned to admiration. He, too, had a deep love for Jesus Crucified and felt an attraction to the cross. But he had put these yearnings aside in recent months.

The two became fast friends and soon Francis was stopping by the hermitage whenever he went hunting on the mountain. Sometimes when he didn't feel like shooting, he would hike up to the cave just to talk with Spada.

By contrast, the people Francis was meeting at parties seemed to have all the money they wanted and no cares at all. His father insisted he visit the Pannechettis more often, and the two families appeared to take it for granted that he and Maria were engaged. Even though there was no formal announcement of the fact, it seemed just a matter of time.

Occasionally, too, Francis went on business trips with his father, and each journey was a new adventure. Dining with Sante was always interesting, for he knew what to order and how it should be prepared. The wines and liqueurs and champagnes that he insisted on having were new and exhilarating to Checchino. He had been acquainted only with Pacifica's homemade wine and the local vintages of the valley. Now he was seeing how others lived.

Sometimes Sante would call him into his study and discuss with him a case pending in the courts, or ask his advice on a piece of business. Then he would nod approval at Checchino's sagacity, or painstakingly correct some imprudent suggestion.

While the Congress of Paris was in session during March of 1856, Sante had long talks with his son about the political situation, in which the delegate from Sardinia, the crafty Count Cavour, was causing the Holy See grave concern. It was an open secret that he was urging Louis Napoleon to aid Sardinia in expelling Austria from the peninsula and creating a free and united people.

"It all sounds well and good," Sante pointed out, "to talk about a free and united Italy. But any such unification is an indirect attack on the Holy Father and will deprive him of his temporal power. Christ's representative on earth cannot be subject to any temporal power! He must be free and independent of any political ties!"

Francis fervently agreed.

He was busy with his schoolwork, heavier social life, and occasional trips, and the Passionists were hardly ever in his thoughts of late. It was all studies, sports, and friends.

One afternoon while riding south of town Francis caught sight of a chicken hawk floating on lazy wings near the abandoned Church of San Pietro. He slipped off the horse, took his gun from his saddle holster, and stealthily maneuvered for a closer shot. Ahead of him was a little hillside stream. As he tried to jump it, his foot slipped on the muddy bank and he fell with the cocked gun in his hands. The hammer snapped, the gun roared and Francis felt a searing pain across his face. He lay there, his ears ringing, terror-stricken, numbly wondering what had happened. When he put his hand to his face, he could feel the blood trickling down. Grabbing his handkerchief he held it to his nose.

Fortunately, only a single piece of shot had torn the flesh across his nose; the rest of the blast had missed him by a fraction of an inch. If it had been any closer it would have blinded him . . . perhaps killed him. When he reflected on the accident later, he realized that Providence had spared him. But for what? Was his narrow escape intended to remind him of a higher vocation?

As the first anniversary of the town's deliverance from

the cholera drew near, the townspeople joined in preparations for the great procession they had vowed. The octave day of the Assumption, August 22, dawned bright and calm.

The procession was scheduled for three o'clock in the afternoon, and an hour before that the great cannons of *La Rocca* began booming a salute to the Madonna. Then followed the ringing of the bells in all fifty-nine churches of Spoleto. Everybody, dressed in gala attire, flocked to the cathedral and overflowed the piazza. The whole place was gay with decorations, and an orchestra poured forth sacred music from the doors of the Opera House. Great silken tapestries and rich damask hung from the windows around the square, and garlands of fresh blossoms were festooned from balcony to balcony.

Sante Possenti, because of his city office, walked in the procession. Canon Spasvoli had had the servers draw lots for their appointments and Francis missed out. Accordingly, he took a place at the edge of the crowd, on the southeast corner of the piazza, where the icon procession would turn back to the cathedral.

The great doors of the cathedral swung open and the procession began. First came the acolytes with lighted tapers and swinging censers. Next followed Sante Possenti walking with the governor of Spoleto and the city council. Behind them came the canons of the cathedral in their bright red cassocks, preceding four deacons in gold-brocaded dalmatics who held aloft on a flower-festooned platform, the great icon in its rich reliquary. Last of all, with two chaplains, came Archbishop Arnaldi robed in a cope of gold lamé and wearing a jeweled miter.

At the sight of the icon a triumphant shout of joy and

praise went up from thousands of throats, and the piazza filled with their cries: *"Viva Maria! Viva nostra Madonna!"*

Slowly the procession moved around the great square, as clergy and people sang hymns to Mary, whose intercession had delivered them from the cholera. A thrill of exultation swept through Francis.

As the picture was carried past the spot where he was kneeling, his eyes met those of the icon. Then came one of the decisive moments of his life. It seemed to him that the eyes of the Virgin Mother became alive and peered into the deepest recesses of his soul. He suddenly felt caught in a mysterious force which he was powerless to resist. As he gazed spellbound, although the lips of the icon did not move, in the depths of his soul he heard a voice which said: "Francis, why do you remain in the world? It is not for you. Follow your vocation!"

It was the act of a moment, but in that moment the whole course of his life was changed. The procession moved slowly on. But Francis remained kneeling, dazed by the grace that had illumined his soul. His conscience had been laid bare, and he realized his unfaithfulness. He had been toying with the grace of his vocation, but Mary had won for him another chance.

Tears came to his eyes, and as soon as Benediction was over, he slipped away from the crowd and walked thoughtfully over to the Jesuit college to see his confessor, Father Bompiani. "Did this experience," he wondered, "come from the emotional excitement of the procession, or from a special action of the Holy Spirit?"

"It is from God," Father Bompiani assured him, "and I would urge you to make application to the Passionists without further delay!"

CHAPTER III

THE YEAR IS OVER

> "Rise up . . . for after a year the vintage
> is ready and there shall be no more
> gathering." (Isa. 32:9.)

When Francis returned home that evening, he found his father sitting alone, reading the paper.

"I went to see Father Bompiani about joining the Passionists," Checchino stated. "He's in favor of my making application immediately."

Sante looked up sharply and the paper slipped from his hands. Suddenly he rose and going to the window drew the curtains and looked out intently, as if there were something to see outside in the gathering gloom.

"You say he approved?" he said, not turning his head.

"Yes, and he recommended that I write tonight. You'll give your blessing, won't you?"

Sante turned to his son and Francis noticed even in his confusion that there was no anger in his father's eyes. It was like the bored look he had once seen on his face as they had watched together the last act of a none-too-amusing comedy.

"I could never approve a son of mine joining a group like the Passionists," he said quietly, emphatically. "The diocese, yes . . . for then one day your talents and abilities would be recognized. I would even consider the Jesuits . . . but those Passionists, never! In my judgment they are simply pious peasants!"

"No, Papa! You're mistaken." Francis leaped to his feet and running to his father caught his arm. "They are a wonderful group of missionaries — I — " He stopped for he could find no other words.

Sante put his hand under his son's chin. Quietly he turned his face up to the light and looked for an intent moment into his eyes. The boy looked back at him, his heart in his eyes, his lips quivering as he tried to find in his father's face some answering emotion, some sign of hope, of joy. Surely he must approve. But the inscrutable expression which had baffled him so often was all that his frantic, searching eyes could find.

Slowly Sante withdrew his hand. He walked back to his chair and sprawled tiredly, his chin on his chest, his eyes looking up at his son from under heavy lids.

"You are wrong about the Passionists," Francis began again, finding words. "Father, this afternoon, during the procession, I suddenly knew for sure. . . ."

"You are tired son," the old man answered, still watching him. "We'll talk about it tomorrow."

"But I must tell you!"

"Francis," he said heavily, "I don't want to hear — anything."

"But you don't know what I'm going to say!"

"Son, it's written plainly on your face. Something or someone has convinced you that you should be a Passionist, and," he sighed slightly, "I don't intend to argue about it. We'll talk about it later."

The next morning when Francis came downstairs, he found his father waiting for him. He looked anxiously at the old man. If only he would say yes! If only he would hold out his arms, so he could run to him, as he had done so often as a child. But Sante looked drained, as if he hadn't slept the whole night.

"Checchino," he began, "once I had such brilliant plans for you. But they don't matter any more."

"Don't matter? What are you talking about? Of course, they matter! Papa, you will let me go, won't you?"

"There's nothing I can do about it. If your mind is made up, you might as well go."

Francis impulsively threw his arms around his father and tried to tell him the gratitude that welled in his heart. But the joy was not mutual. The old man patted his son's shoulder listlessly and remarked, "Pacifica is waiting. Let's go in to breakfast."

Later that morning Francis wrote to the Very Reverend Father Simon, provincial of the Passionists, making formal application for admission and giving the name of Father Bompiani for reference. He addressed the letter to the provincial house at Recanati and waited anxiously for an answer. Within a week there was delivered to his home a favorable reply, explaining that if he obtained the necessary papers he could be accepted for the next class at the novitiate. But Francis never saw the letter. Sante intercepted it and kept it from his son.

When two weeks had passed and Francis had heard nothing, he began to wonder what was wrong. Two of his classmates, Caesar Caladrelli and Ponziano Grismondi, who had decided on the Passionists during the annual student retreat, and had made application and been accepted. They planned to leave for the novitiate before the commencement exercises.

A thousand conjectures crowded Francis' mind. Maybe the letter had been lost in the mails? Or maybe Father Simon was away? Or could it be that he had the wrong address? But one thought was dominant: "I'm going to enter regardless. . . . They'll have to close the door in my face, if they don't want me!"

From Caesar and Ponziano he learned all the preliminary details. First, he had to get an affidavit from his parish priest attesting to the fact that he was single and of good morals. Then this affidavit had to be certified by one of the priests at the chancery office. Next, he had to secure a certificate from the civil and police authorities, granting him permission to leave the city and to reside elsewhere.

Francis obtained these documents, but still had heard nothing from Father Simon. The time was getting short. He sent a second letter and quietly resolved to follow his classmates to the Passionist novitiate even if he didn't get an answer.

Two weeks later the commencement exercises were held at the Jesuit college. Francis would have preferred to miss the excitement of this event as his two classmates were doing, but he had been chosen to give the valedictory address and his teachers were relying on him to make a good showing. Moreover, he had two special awards coming and it would be a proud moment for his father to see him receive these honors.

The day before graduation his two older brothers, Louis and Michael, came home for the celebration. Sante told them about Francis' wild idea of joining the Passionists. "I want you both to speak to him," he said. "Try to make him see the foolishness of such a stunt."

It was agreed that Louis, a Dominican priest known by the name of Father Aloysius, should be the first to speak. He found Francis in his room, and said to him, "I don't think you realize, Checchino, the sorrow you've caused Papa. I doubt if you have any idea of the rigors of the Passionists. They are far stricter than the Dominicans, and many times you have said that we have too hard a rule."

Francis grinned. "I bet Papa sent you up here to talk to me."

Louis blushed involuntarily. This young brother of his had a sharpness he had not remembered. He had seen through those solicitous remarks.

"So what?" Louis asked with a laugh, and then lapsed into silence.

"Father Aloysius," Francis began deferentially. "This is something I have had on my mind for a long time. Do you remember what happened about five years ago, when I had that terrible throat infection?"

Louis recalled the afternoon Francis had returned from school complaining of a sore throat. It was shortly after Easter, while he was home for the holidays. Everyone had dismissed the ailment as a case of laryngitis, due perhaps to a cold. But during the night the inflammation grew worse. Next morning Checchino had come downstairs slowly, feeling faint, clinging to the banister to keep from falling. His legs were trembling with weakness and he shivered from the clammy sweat that covered his body.

Feebly he made his way to the kitchen and collapsed in the arms of Maria Louise.

Louis had helped his sister carry Francis back to bed, while Vincent was sent running for the doctor. As they waited for the physician, Maria tried to comfort Checchino, and Louis remembered pulling the shades to shut out the heat and brightness of the morning sun.

When Doctor Mariani arrived, he diagnosed the condition immediately. "It's a case of quinsy," he said, "similar to the one he had a couple years ago. Only this time it is more serious. His whole larynx is inflamed and it looks like a huge puss-sack is forming on the left side. But I don't dare lance it now. If it is not ripe, it will only spread the infection. I'll swab it with some medicine. Then all we can do is wait and pray. Keep the boy quiet, and don't give him anything except a little watered wine. His condition is critical."

As the day wore on, Louis remembered how he had sat at Checchino's bedside, fanning him and putting damp cloths on his fevered brow. Sante had gone to the court, but he returned an hour later to watch at the bedside.

At first Francis had wanted to hold his brother's hand when the pain was bad, but he clamped down so hard that Louis had to switch from one to the other. Finally, he had knotted two long towels together, tied them to the foot of the bed and put the knotted ends in Checchino's hands. He would never forget how his brother had hung onto them as though they were lifelines, straining and slacking. Occasionally he dropped the towels to put his hands to his throat and looked at those around the bed, his eyes enormous with pain.

Hours dragged by. The clock in the room had stopped, but they all knew that the day was waning. The heat lessened and the bright pinpoints of light through the shade grew duller.

Checchino seemed about the same, and there was little the family could do for him. They went down to dinner, assuring him that they would be back as soon as they were finished.

"While you and the others were downstairs," Francis explained now to his brother, "it seemed my whole life passed before me. I thought I was dying . . . and what had I accomplished? Nothing! I've never told this to any of the family before, but in that moment I promised our heavenly Mother that if she saved me, I would become a priest. I would let nothing stop me!"

Father Aloysius nodded reflectively, as Francis continued: "Right after I made this promise, I reached for a picture of Blessed Andrew Bobola, which was on the table at my bedside. It was a holy card Father Bompiani had given me on the occasion of Andrew's beatification. As I looked at that picture, I remembered that this Jesuit martyr had had his tongue torn out with pincers. On a sudden impulse I clutched it to my throat. 'Blessed Andrew,' I pleaded, 'help me!'

"Suddenly the pus sack broke and I started to spit out the poison. I wanted to call you, but my throat was too swollen. As I lay there waiting for you to return, the pain seemed to leave me and a great weariness enveloped me. My eyes closed and I fell asleep. Next morning, as you remember, both the pain and the inflammation were gone. I knew that Blessed Andrew Bobola had cured me . . . and that I owed it to Mary to become a priest."

"Did you do anything about it?" Louis questioned.

"Yes, I saw Father Bernard Rossi, the provincial of the Jesuits, and asked admission into the Society. He checked with my spiritual director, Father Tedeschini, then sent a letter of acceptance. I probably would have entered the Society had I not meanwhile attended Passionist missions at our parish church and the cathedral. What I there observed so attracted me to these missionaries that I wanted to become like them."

"If I recall rightly," Father Aloysius commented, "the Passionists have given several other missions here in Spoleto."

"Yes, seven — and I made every one of them!"

Louis had listened solemnly to the story and heard with amazement the well-ordered and explicit reasons Francis had for becoming a Passionist. Finally, the younger brother asked:

"Now what do you think?"

"Checchino, I believe you are right. This is not a whim. You have a true vocation and you must follow it. No one should oppose it."

Francis was, of course, delighted at these words. His older brother's influence would be helpful with their father.

Later Michael, who was studying medicine, unaware that Checchino had won over Louis, tried his luck. "Tell me, Checchino," he began, "is it true that you have made up your mind to become a Passionist?"

"Yes. And what about it?"

"Have you thought the matter over well?"

"Certainly!" he snapped. "I've taken a lot longer than you did in deciding to become a doctor!"

Michael winced. Francis was throwing him on the defensive. He still wasn't sure he wanted to go on with his studies. He had been thinking of becoming a priest himself, but he had done nothing about it. A little chagrined Michael decided to let the matter drop.

Since neither of the boys had made Francis reconsider, Sante decided that the matter should be handled quickly and quietly. Father Aloysius would accompany him to the novitiate at Morrovale, and if anyone asked where they were going, they could say that they were going to visit relatives and make a pilgrimage to nearby Loreto. Then, if Checchino should change his mind or find that the Passionists were not to his liking, he could return home without causing gossip. Accordingly, tickets were purchased for the trip to Loreto and reservations made on the coach for the morning of September 6.

Commencement day was a busy one for Francis. After Mass he went to the Opera House for rehearsals and to practice his speech. Then he went out of his way to visit the Church of St. Luke, which had been one of his favorite shrines to the Blessed Virgin. He wanted to thank his heavenly Mother for having won for him such a great favor. On the way home he stopped at the little Oratory of San Angelo to kneel in prayer before the tomb of his earthly mother and his sister Adele. The names of both were carved upon the same headstone, for they had died only a week apart.

Francis hardly remembered Adele, but he could never forget his mother. She had taken sick at the end of January, 1842, shortly after they had moved to Spoleto from his birthplace in Assisi. The doctor had said she died of meningitis, but that wasn't the full story. Agnes Possenti had worn herself out in caring for her family. Then losing two children in two months was more than she could stand. Her heart seemed broken.

Though he was only four at the time, he remembered the excitement of her death. It was on the evening of February 8 that she took a turn for the worse. One of the older boys was sent for the priest; another ran for the doctor. After Father Bernardine had given her the sacraments, she rolled her head to one side and lay looking intently at his father while her features sharpened. Everyone in the sickroom held his breath, feeling sure she would speak before she died. And she did.

With a painful smile and a clicking of breath in her mouth, she murmured, "The children . . . my babies. . . ."

Each stepped up in turn and kissed their mother's fevered cheeks. She seemed too weak to say anything more, but when Francis had leaned over to kiss her, she whispered, "May Mary keep you, my Checchino!"

Surely his heavenly Mother had heard that prayer and was sending him to the Passionists.

Since he might never again see Spoleto, he decided that afternoon to complete the rounds by riding out to the cemetery of San Salvatore to visit the grave of Maria Louise. As he knelt over the mound which enclosed all that remained on earth of his dearest sister, tears filled his eyes at the memory of her many kindnesses to him.

The day after his mother's death, he recalled, he had run through the house, crying, "*Mama mia . . . mama mia!*" Maria Louise, overcome with grief herself, had gathered him into her arms and tried to comfort him. "I will be your mama, Checchino. I will take care of you."

Maria Louise had kept her word . . . and more. Now

in heaven she surely knew about his vocation and rejoiced with him.

At the graduation ceremony that evening the Opera
House was filled with parents, friends, and relatives of the
graduates. The clergy and civil authorities were also present, for the Jesuit college was the center of learning in
Spoleto. The annual commencement was an event which
concerned the whole city. In the place of honor sat the
apostolic delegate, Monsignor Guadalupi, and at either
side, Archbishop Arnaldi and Sante Possenti.

When it came time for his address, Francis stood erect
and flawlessly groomed before his audience, his dark eyes
flashing with the secret fire that glowed within his soul.
On this night of nights he wanted to do his very best,
and he succeeded well. As he finished, amid much applause, Monsignor Guadalupi leaned over to Sante and
whispered, "If your son were here beside me, I would
take him in my arms and embrace him!"

When it came time to bestow the honors and diplomas,
the apostolic delegate went out of his way to congratulate
Francis Possenti. "You have great talents, young man, and
I hope you use them for the honor and glory of God and
the service of your fellowman." The prelate then decorated
him with a special gold medal for excellence in philosophy
and proficiency in the classics — the two most coveted
honors bestowed by the college. His classmates joined
enthusiastically in the applause, for Francis was a general
favorite.

Waiting in the audience to congratulate him was Maria
Pannechetti with her parents. The judge was loud in his
praise of the young man and insisted that Sante and his
son come over to his house for a little celebration. "After

all," he remarked with a knowing wink, "our families could hardly be closer."

Francis could not refuse this hospitality and he did drop in for a short visit. Maria commented later that when he left that night she had the feeling she would never see him again.

At home there was another party with some of his classmates and friends. He spent more than an hour with Philip Giovannetti, then slipped outside with Peter Parenzi. The two walked up and down the piazza in front of the house until one-thirty in the morning. Peter remarked later, "I knew there was something on Checchino's mind, but he wouldn't tell me. We just reminisced about our youth together and the good times we had had. When I suggested going in, he kept detaining me. 'Let's walk just a little longer, Peter. I have so much to tell you!'"

When finally the two friends returned to the house, the party was breaking up. Francis quickly retired to his room and wrote a long letter to Peter, putting down all the things he had not had the courage to tell him personally. When at length he went to bed, sleep would not come. He tossed fitfully until dawn.

He was up early to pack the single bag he was taking. There was a tearful farewell with Pacifica to whom he entrusted the care of his pieta. "Keep a vigil light in front of it," he entreated her, "and don't forget to pray for me. I'll send notes to you when I write father, so you won't forget." Then he kissed her.

Sante walked with his son to the coach, holding Checchino's arm tightly in his own. As they embraced for the last time, tears flooded Francis' eyes.

The brothers boarded the coach which already had four

passengers: Father Mario Speranza, a parish priest of Spoleto, and two children with their governess. Francis climbed up with the driver, where it wouldn't be so crowded riding, and where he would have a better look at the town and countryside he was seeing for the last time.

The sun was just beginning to peep over the rim of the valley as the coach rolled down the cobblestoned streets, crossed the Torrente Tessino, and headed northeast on the Flaminian Way.

CHAPTER IV

"DON'T ASK ME TO LEAVE!"

> *"No one, having put his hand to the plow
> and looking back, is fit for the kingdom
> of God."* (Lk. 9:62.)

Morrovale, site of the Passionist novitiate, is a quaint little town situated on the eastern foothills of the Apennines, within sight of the Adriatic Sea. It lies about eighty miles northeast of Spoleto and is reached by taking the Flaminian Way north to Foligno and then turning east on the winding road to Tolentino and Macerata.

Francis and his brother, however, went by way of Loreto, which is sixteen miles farther north, so they might visit the *Santa Casa,* or "Holy House," which is preserved there. A pious tradition more than six centuries old maintains that the little stone building within the great Basilica of Loreto is the one in which the Holy Family lived at Nazareth.

On the way to this shrine Francis was happy and frequently burst into song. The sun that shone down upon him was warm and tender, the air was fragrant, and the glory of summer was spread before his eyes. Along the roadside the blackberry brambles had been picked clean of fruit by the meadowlarks, and the bare granite boulders pushing up through the brown earth were draped with wild roses and surrounded with lavender periwinkles.

All morning Francis was in an exuberant mood, but by noon he was quite tired. During the afternoon he rode inside the coach, napping occasionally.

At sundown the coach stopped at the village of Muccia. The two brothers were able to get a hot meal, but their beds were plain straw mats. Father Aloysius jokingly remarked that they were getting a taste of Passionist austerity.

"I don't mind," Francis replied. "I'm so tired I could sleep anywhere."

Next morning they were off early, hoping to get to Loreto before evening. They rode through Tolentino without stopping and passed Macerata about noon. At Recanati, where they stopped for lunch, they could see the dome of the Basilica of Loreto far down on the marshes. It stood on a promontory in a large stand of laurels, from which it is said to have received its name. In the hazy distance could be seen the blue of the Adriatic.

After lunch they resumed their journey. A stiff wind was blowing in from the sea and the clouds overhead had turned the color of slate. As they neared Loreto a violent thundershower broke upon them. The driver refused to go on, so they turned off the road and sought shelter in a nearby stable, where they waited out the storm.

When the journey was resumed, darkness was falling. Despite the bad weather, they found there were many pilgrims in town and all the inns were filled. The Possenti brothers were forced to accept the only accommodations left, straw mattresses stretched out in the hallway of the hospice, which faced on the *Piazza della Santa Casa*.

That evening they visited their maternal uncle, Monsignor Caesar Acquacotta. He was the most important ecclesiastic in town, being both a canon of the basilica and vicar-general of the diocese. His residence was attached to the convent of nuns on Monte Reale, where he also served as chaplain.

It was a happy surprise to the prelate to see his two nephews, and he welcomed them heartily, insisting they stay for dinner. However, his quarters were so small he could not keep them overnight.

As they were leaving, Father Aloysius took his uncle aside and slipped him a letter from Sante Possenti. "Father asked me to give this to you," he said. "It's about my brother and the plan he has to become a Passionist. Perhaps you can advise him."

"We'll see," Monsignor Acquacotta murmured noncommittally. Years of service in the chancery office at Macerata had taught him to be wary of delicate issues.

When they returned to the hospice, Francis noticed that a window at the end of the hallway looked out on the basilica. He carried his mattress over to it and sat for a long time looking at the sanctuary. The storm was passing. To the left of the great dome the moon intermittently broke through the clouds, turning the wet piazza into a sea of misty light.

It was a place for reverie, and Francis' thoughts wandered back over the past and then into the future. He knew that he had left broken hearts behind and that for some the world would never be the same without him. He also realized that if he had delayed any longer, his own heart would have been so ensnared he would never have left home. He felt a tremendous peace within himself, though every now and then a wave of loneliness and fear surged up from the depths of his being, filling him with a vague sense of regret. Was he being too heroic? Would he have the strength to persevere? What if the Passionists didn't accept him?

He whispered a prayer, blessed himself, and lay down on his straw mat. However, there were so many pilgrims coming and going in the hallway that sleep was impossible. The two brothers tossed most of the night.

The next morning, September 8, they rose very early and went over to the basilica. It was the Feast of the Nativity of the Blessed Virgin, but hardly anyone was abroad at that hour. Francis served his brother's Mass at the altar within the Holy House and received Communion. After a short thanksgiving they went over to the Jesuit house, where they found two of their former professors from the college in Spoleto. The fathers gave them a most cordial welcome and served them breakfast.

When they returned to the basilica, there was still an hour or more before the solemn Mass. One of the Capuchin fathers, custodians of the sanctuary, was sitting in his confessional. Francis decided to take advantage of the opportunity and made a general confession of his whole life. He did so with such exactness that he never felt the need to repeat it. In turn, it brought him great consolation and peace of mind.

He was still kneeling in prayer in the Holy House, when his brother came to remind him that Mass was about to start in the main part of the basilica. "Let's hurry," Father Aloysius whispered, "and get a place near the high altar."

"No," Francis answered. "I'd rather stay here. I'll see you later."

"You'll miss the pontifical Mass! Our uncle will be on for services!"

"I don't care. I want to stay here."

As Francis Possenti knelt in worshipful silence before the age-blackened image of the Virgin and her Child, he reflected that in this very house Mary had made possible the salvation of the world by answering the Angel Gabriel: "Behold the handmaid of the Lord! Be it done to me according to Thy word!" In the same spot he now begged her for the grace to utter his own *fiat*.

By the time his brother returned for him, Francis' soul was flooded with peace and happiness.

That afternoon the brothers went a second time to dine with their uncle. By this time Monsignor Acquacotta had had a chance to read Sante's letter. He found himself in complete sympathy with it. The Passionists were too strict, not the type at all for his nephew.

The meal was scarcely over before the prelate launched into his subject. "Tell me, Checchino," he began, "what made you think of the Passionists?"

Francis bit his lip in embarrassment. He realized what was coming.

Without waiting for an answer, Monsignor Acquacotta proceeded to portray vividly the rigors and austerities of life among the followers of Paul of the Cross. He also admitted that as a young man he had spent a short time in a Passionist novitiate, and from personal experiences had found the rule too strict.

"Don't you think I should at least try?" Francis questioned quietly.

"Listen, Checchino," the Monsignor continued emphatically, "the romantic ideas you have about solitude and penance will vanish very quickly when you are brought face to face with the cold, hard rule which imposes continual mortification and self-denial. The straw mattress, chanting the Office in the middle of the night, the rough habit, the long fast will soon dispel this fancy that has bewitched you. Then you will be more than glad to return to the kind of life to which you have become accustomed."

"But I'm convinced it's my vocation," Francis interrupted.

"It's so unreasonable!" the Monsignor continued, shaking his head.

Francis started to answer sharply, but caught himself. After all, his uncle was a man of experience and position. He had to respect him, even if he didn't agree with him.

Seeing the obdurate look on his nephew's face, the Monsignor tried another tack. "If you go through with this plan," he said, "you will be making it hard on yourself and us. Think of the embarrassment it will cause when you return home. Your father won't be able to hold up his head when people ask about you. To them you will be a failure. Worst of all, your friends won't let you forget this abortive piety. They'll consider it one big joke!"

Francis answered in a steady voice: "Monsignor, I have thought long and often of all that you have told me. I have weighed it well. I am convinced that God has given me a vocation to this life and I have no alternative but to accept. If I am generous with God, He will give me the grace to persevere. It would be an even greater disgrace to you and the family, if I became a coward and turned back!"

Monsignor Acquacotta threw up his hands in defeat and turned to Father Aloysius. "Tell your father," he said, "that I did my best!"

Next morning at eight the brothers left by carriage for Civitanova, some fourteen miles directly south of Loreto. They planned to walk from there to Morrovale.

As they rode down the tree-lined road that runs along the coast of the Adriatic, Father Aloysius mentioned that they would have to stop and see their aunt and uncle in Civitanova. They hadn't seen the Frisciottis since their mother's funeral.

"All right," Francis replied, "but the visit will have to be brief."

As the carriage rolled into the little seaport town to which Sante Possenti had been sent as governor by Pope Pius VII in 1814, Francis noticed landmarks of which he had heard his father speak: the Church of St. Marone, where Sante and Agnes had been married, and the government building where his father had presided for seven years.

The Frisciotti's welcomed the brothers heartily. Aunt Elena immediately began to make grandiose plans for the next few days. And, they just couldn't go on to Morrovale.

"Morrovale is such a lonely place back in the hills," she exclaimed. "You should hear the dreadful stories going around about those monks. They sleep on straw like peasants and walk barefooted. Surely, my dears, you're not going to stay there long."

Francis gracefully evaded a definite answer then, but

after dinner his uncle pried from him an admission that he planned to join the Passionists. A futile argument followed. Checchino remained courteous, but the visit upset him. He did not regain his composure until he was again on the way to Morrovale.

The Passionist novitiate is a little more than six miles due west of Civitanova, on a small hill north of the town of Morrovale. The road the brothers took wound around and through the town, then down a little ravine formed by a tributary of the Chienti River, and up the farther side. On the right was a Capuchin monastery and farther on the Passionist retreat. Built in 1789, it was the first house founded after the death of St. Paul of the Cross. Its first superior had been St. Vincent Mary Strambi, later bishop of Macerata.

As they drew near the two monasteries, Francis was elated. He wanted to hurry directly to the Passionists, but Father Aloysius reminded him that another uncle of theirs, Father John Baptist Frisciotti, was guardian of the Capuchin monastery, and would it be unthinkable to pass him by without a visit. Moreover, Sante had written a letter to him also, which Father Aloysius was to deliver. Resignedly, therefore, Francis turned in at the Capuchin Monastery and waited while Father Aloysius rang the porter's bell. A lay brother ushered them into the small parlor, where they were soon joined by their uncle.

Father John Baptist Frisciotti, O.F.M.Cap., a short man with a heavy brown beard that matched his ample brown habit, smiled happily at the sight of his visitors and enveloped both in a tremendous embrace.

Then picking up their bags he invited them back to the guest rooms. Francis tried to demur: "We're not staying," he insisted. "I'm on my way to the Passionists."

"Nonsense!" Father John Baptist replied. "I wouldn't think of letting you go over there this evening. You must stay and have supper with me. I haven't seen the two of you for so long and there is so much I want to hear about your family. A poor host I'd be to turn you out without a meal!"

The room into which he took Francis was one of the usual type kept for guests. It had about it a musty odor compounded of stale incense and furniture polish. He thought it was sort of a "religious" smell. His uncle unlatched the shutters and pushed open the window.

"Make yourself comfortable," he admonished, "and I'll be back as soon as I get your brother settled."

Father John Baptist went out, shutting the door, and Francis sat down on the bed dejectedly, listening to the only sound in the monastery — the soft shuffle of his uncle's sandals retreating down the corridor.

He went over to the table on which was a book with a faded brown cover, entitled "Confessions of St. Augustine." Idly he turned the pages, remembering the day when as a student at college he had first read that autobiography. Here and there he noticed scribblings made by previous occupants of the room. "Holy Mary, pray for me!" he read on one page. On another, written in blotched ink, as though the writer's tears had splashed down on the script, were the words, "I am a miserable sinner — have mercy on me!" He closed the book with the unpleasant feeling that he had been eavesdropping.

He wondered what could be keeping Father John Baptist. Then he remembered the letter his father had entrusted to his brother. That would be it! His uncle had read the letter and the two were no doubt discussing him, perhaps even now planning the strategy of another assault on his resolution.

After a few minutes there was a knock on the door and Father John Baptist walked in without waiting for an answer. "I was just reading a letter from your father," he began quite candidly, "and he tells me that your health is much too frail for the austerities of the Passionist life. From the looks of you I'm inclined to agree."

Arguing about the rigorous life of the Passionists was beginning to bore Francis. Everyone seemed to think that the sons of Paul of the Cross were inhuman. Yet hundreds of young men like himself were living happily in their retreats. If they could do it, so could he!

"Take my habit, for example," Father John Baptist continued, holding up his sleeve for examination. "If you think this robe is heavy, you ought to see the coarse ones the Passionists wear!"

With one argument after the other his uncle tested him. Most objections he refuted with a smile, but to his uncle's questions, he gave clear and firm replies. Finally, Father John Baptist was convinced of the boy's sincerity and called a truce.

The brothers remained with their uncle until the afternoon of Sept 10. Then he walked with them the short distance to the Passionist novitiate. On the way the two priests spoke of going the next day to Monte Giorgio to see their relative, Sister Maria Teresa Frisciotti. This Augustinian nun was their mother's only sister, and Father John Baptist mentioned that she was not well and probably wouldn't live much longer. It would certainly cheer the old nun to see her two nephews. Checchino said nothing, but walked on with his eyes fixed ahead for the first sight of his new home.

As they came over a little rise, he caught a glimpse of the belfry of the church dedicated to Our Lady of the Oaks. Then the red tiles and white walls of the monastery came into full view.

They went directly to the retreat entrance and Francis pulled the rope at the portal. The bell clanged in the cloister, and after a few moments the door opened and Brother Camillus smilingly invited them into the small, unadorned reception room. They identified themselves and asked to see the novice master.

As Brother Camillus withdrew, Father John Baptist commented, "Did you notice how gracious and respectful that porter was? He was trained at court. Before joining the Passionists he was valet to Cardinal Prince di Belvedere."

Francis paid little attention to his uncle, but sat down on one of the straight-backed chairs that stood against the wall and tried to be calm. A sudden cold fright seemed to have fallen upon him. What if they wouldn't accept him? After all his insistence in coming . . . what if they turned him away? If his heart would only stop pounding in his ears, perhaps he could think of what to do. But the quick thudding only increased when he heard the patter of sandaled feet coming down the corridor.

The door opened and in came a black-robed religious, a slender man with white hair and an extremly firm jaw. Father Raphael of St. Anthony, master of novices, was not one to stand on ceremony. He had no time for the polite circumlocutions with which people generally begin their conversations. He came directly to the point: "We had practically given up hope of seeing you, Francis. When you didn't answer Father Provincial's invitation, I thought you had changed your mind. So many young men write, asking admission, and then at the last minute lose courage."

"Did Father Simon write?" Francis exclaimed. "I received no letter."

Father Aloysius felt embarrassed, suddenly realizing that his father must have held back this letter. But he marveled the more at his brother's insistence on coming without even knowing that he would be welcome.

"Yes," Father Raphael continued. "The provincial told me last week that he had written you, accepting you for the novitiate and telling you when to report here. He also listed the affidavits you needed and mentioned that twenty-eight florins would cover the cost of a habit — "

"My brother has his papers and sufficient money," Father Aloysius cut in, hoping to change the subject. "I'm sure everything will be all right."

"Then the next thing," said Father Raphael rising, "is to get our new postulant settled." He excused himself for a moment and returned with his assistant, Father Norbert Cassinelli.

The vice-master was a young man, rather short in stature, and slender almost to emaciation. His eyes were dark, keen and penetrating, and his features well defined, as if carved from ivory. The austerity of his presence, however, was relieved by a tender and sensitive mouth and the smile that lingered about his lips made Francis feel that he would be a sympathetic friend.

As the vice-master invited Francis to follow him to his room in the novitiate, the rector of the monastery came in with a pitcher of beer, some cheese and bread. He greeted the new postulant with a warm smile and then turned his attention to the two priest visitors. "There's nothing like a refreshing glass of beer on a warm afternoon," he exclaimed jovially, "and here at the novitiate we always welcome a chance to entertain. We don't get visitors very often."

Father Norbert led Francis to a neat little room in the middle of the third floor corridor. This was to be Francis' monastic "cell." It was fourteen feet long and twelve feet wide, furnished with a bed with a straw mattress covered with a white sheet, a pillow and brown woolen blanket; a table and two straight-backed chairs. On the whitewashed walls hung a crucifix and two sacred pictures. The window looked to the east, and in the distance Francis could see the blue haze of the Adriatic. Directly below was the vegetable garden and, a little way beyond, a chicken coop.

He put down his hat and bag and followed Father Norbert to the recreation room at the end of the corridor. By that mysterious telegraphy proper to religious institutes, everyone in the novitiate knew that a new postulant had arrived and they were waiting to meet him. As Francis was introduced, he tried to keep the names straight and to fix them in his memory. There was Father Bernard Mary; Confrater Anthony; Vincent; Alexander; two classmates from the Jesuit college, Caesar and Ponziano; and two brother novices, Leonard and Joseph. After a few minutes of pleasant banter, they returned to the parlor.

While Francis had been gone, his uncle and brother had arranged with the rector for him to return to the Capuchin monastery that evening. The next morning all three were to visit Sister Maria Teresa.

Francis objected strenuously, when he heard of their plan. "Don't ask me to leave! I can see Sister Maria Teresa some other time. I want to stay here!"

His uncle showed his disappointment and his brother shrugged his shoulders. Father Raphael smiled to himself. It augured well for the new postulant.

Father John Baptist gave his nephew a fond farewell and promised to return soon. Then the brothers embraced affectionately. Father Aloysius' lip trembled with emotion.

"Embrace Papa for me," Francis murmured, "and give my love to the others." He looked down to hide a tear that welled up in the corner of his eye.

The visitors then shook hands with the rector and departed. As they walked slowly down the road, Father Aloysius turned to his uncle and remarked sadly, "Somehow I have the feeling I'll never see Checchino again."

Closest possible likeness of Gabriel Francis Possenti, obtained from painting over an old tintype. Original is hung in office of Bishop Batistelli, C.P., Teramo, Italy.

View of the Possenti home in Spoleto,
where St. Gabriel spent most of his childhood.

Father
Sante Possenti

Mother
Agnes Possenti

Monte Luco, where St. Gabriel as a boy hunted rabbits and squirrels. The mountain rises about three thousand feet just east of the town of Spoleto.

Cave on Monte Luco, where old man Spada lived as a hermit. On ledge below, St. Gabriel and the old man often sat and talked for hours.

The fortress of La Rocca, as seen from the Piazza Campello, two blocks from the Saint's home.

Main building of the old Jesuit College in Spoleto. It is now used as a military barracks.

Caricatures of his classmates, drawn by St. Gabriel on a page of his copybook while a student at the Jesuit College.

Author with a nephew of St. Gabriel at one of the Saint's favorite picnic spots.

ria Louise Possenti

Teresa Possenti

Dr. Michael Possenti

rior of the opera house, where St.
briel gave his valedictory address
the night of his graduation.

Fr. Louis Possenti, O.P.

View of the Icon Procession, which the people of Spoleto have performed each year since the cholera epidemic of 1856.

Cathedral of Santa Maria Assunta, the *Duomo* of Spolet Here St. Gabriel served as an altar boy. Sometimes during t opera he would slip out of the building at the extreme left to say his rosary, walking back ar forth in the portico.

ine of the Icon inside the
ral. The famous painting
the Madonna can be seen
over the altar.

up of the Icon Procession at the spot where St. Gabriel was
ng when he looked into the face of the Madonna and she
d to say: "Why do you remain in the world?"

Detail photo of the Patronal Madonna of Spoleto. The painting of the Virgin is said to have been done by St. Luke. The stand is overlaid in gold. The crown is studded with diamonds, rubies, and emeralds, while the frame itself is encircled with matched pearls.

Photostat of document Gabriel Francis Possenti needed to get into the Passionist Novitiate. The paragraph at the top is the certification by his pastor that Francis Possenti is single and of good morals. The two signatures on the right-hand side of the page (one above the other) are from the civil and police authorities of Spoleto, giving permission to leave the city. The signature on the left-hand side marks the approbation of the episcopal curia for the affidavit which the pastor has given.

The Passionist Novitiate at Morrovale, Italy. The chapel is
in the center and the entrance to monastery is to the left.

The parlor in the novitiate
at Morrovale. The plastic
tablecloth is the only change
since St. Gabriel's time.

Uncle
Fr. John Baptist
Frisciotti, O.F.M.

Fr. Norbert dell'Orto, C.P.,
Vice-Master and later Di-
rector of St. Gabriel.

Br. Sylvester, C.P., who
nursed St. Gabriel in his
last illness and was present
at his canonization.

The author with a lay brother at
Morrovale, who is about to
leave to collect whatever
generous farmers of the
neighborhood have put aside
for the community.

Copy of the Breviary and Rule Book used by St. Gabriel. Note that there were only two breviaries then for the liturgical year. Also the Saint received a new set, one printed the year of his profession, 1857.

Photostat of page in the Novitiate Ledger, showing Oath of Perseverance, which St. Gabriel made at the end of his novitiate, in which he states that he knows the Rules and Constitutions, and affirms under oath that he has the firm purpose of persevering in the Congregation until death. All is in his own handwriting. Note his signature at the bottom of the page: *Io Confr. Gabriele.*

View of the town of Isola del Gran Sasso, lying below the monastery, with the "great rock" in the background.

View of the monastery at Isola del Gran Sasso, encircled by the mountains.

Main street in the village of Cesa di Francis, where St. Gabriel often went to teach the children catechism.

The statue of the Madonna which St. Gabriel found in an old storeroom. He patched and painted it and made the gown of green velvet. It now stands in a case above the choir altar.

Frs. Natale, Salvatore, Godfrey, and Vincent Mary near the summit of Gran Sasso.

A waxen image of St. Gabriel, wherein his bones are preserved, under the altar of his shrine at Isola del Gran Sasso.

His Holiness, Pope Benedict XV, who canonized Gabriel Francis Possenti and proclaimed "that he should be honored as the new patron of youth throughout the Universal Church."

Front entrance to the Basilica of St. Gabriel at Isola del Gran Sasso. The monastery can be seen behind the church.

View of St. Peter's Basilica, Rome, during the canonization ceremony, May 13, 1920.

CHAPTER V

THE BETTER PART

"Everyone who has left home, or brothers, or sisters, or father . . . for My name's sake, shall receive a hundredfold, and shall possess life everlasting." (Mt. 19:29.)

"This isn't such a penitential place," thought Francis that evening, as he sat down to his first meal in the Passionist novitiate. The table was set with soup, meat and vegetables, wine and fresh fruit. A novice on a raised dais at the end of the room read aloud from a spiritual book, as the religious started eating.

Francis picked up his wooden fork and spoon. "These are like the ones Pacifica used to mix salad," he mused. "I wonder if I'll ever get used to eating with them."

After dinner the novices went into the garden for a short recreation. Naturally, Francis was the center of attention, but he caught himself studying each of them in turn. One was an ordained priest, Father Bernard Mary Silvestrelli, son of a wealthy Roman family. Five others were youths like himself, just out of college. Two candidates for the brotherhood, Leonard and Joseph, were in their late twenties. One came from a farm nearby and the other from the village of Monte Fiori.

All of them were bound together by a common interest and a fraternal charity that constantly bubbled over into innocent banter and good humor. Francis liked the way they kidded one another and the joyous laughter with which they greeted each new sally.

At eight-thirty a bell rang and they all filed into the chapel on the second floor for the evening rosary. Francis knelt in the place assigned him and joined in the invocations with a thankful heart. It seemed like a dream that he was at last in the novitiate, with friends who likewise had consecrated themselves to God. At the end of night prayers a little bell tinkled.

"That's the beginning of the greater silence," a novice whispered to him. "No talking till tomorrow morning."

Francis arose, genuflected, and went to his room. Beneath his window the silent monastery grounds were blotched with the beams of a full moon shining from out over the Adriatic. The great oak trees stood like heavy sentinels on the right, hiding the garden. Ahead in the dim light he could make out an apple orchard. Farther off was a stretch of meadow with several thatched huts where cattle and sheep were housed.

He undressed in the dark and lay down on his straw mattress. It was hard and flat, but he had deliberately asked for this life. He lay there content. At length he fell asleep.

Suddenly a clatter cut across his muddled dreams. It was the Matin rattle, the signal for the religious to rise for the chanting of the night office. The sound was sharp and strident, caused by a wooden clapper like those used in church during Holy week. He sat up in bed and listened. All around him he could hear activity. Novices were rolling out of bed, putting on their sandals, and hurrying to the chapel. He had been told to stay in bed this first night, so he lay back listening and wondering. After a few moments he heard the clapper again, but this time from farther away. Then came the sound of chanting, as the community began the Divine Office.

It was a strange sensation for him to lie there listening to the voices welling up from the chapel below and echoing down the corridor to his room. He had always loved good singing and now thrilled to the tones of Gregorian chant. After a while the chanting receded from his consciousness and he fell asleep.

At six o'clock he was again awakened, this time by the ringing of the monastery bell and the *Angelus*. He got up, dressed, and went down to the chapel. There he assisted at the Office of Prime and Tierce, which was followed by Mass and a period of mental prayer. Afterward he took a simple breakfast of bread and coffee.

The rest of the day was spent in getting acquainted with the routine of the Novitiate. The more he learned of this new life, the more he realized he had made a right choice. Everything about the Passionists thrilled him. He liked their home life, which was patterned so closely on that of the strictest contemplatives. He also liked the missionary apostolate that rivaled the activity of the most modern congregations.

Paul of the Cross, who had founded this new group over a hundred years earlier, had blended both the active and contemplative apostolate in a rule of life which induced Pope Benedict XIV to exclaim: "This congregation is one of the last to be founded in the Church, whereas it should have been the first! One can find nothing better than a life wherein the individual first develops a deep love for Christ Crucified and then through Missions and Retreats develops a similar love in the hearts of the faithful."

On the following day September 14, Francis began a special retreat with the other postulants, Caesar and Ponziano, in preparation for receiving the Passionist habit. The time was divided between prayer and spiritual reading, conferences by Father Salviano, and little domestic duties around the monastery.

Then on the Feast of Our Lady of Sorrows, which that year fell on September 21, he was clothed in the black habit of the Passion. The whole community assembled in the monastery church at nine-thirty in the morning for the ceremony. Father Raphael in surplice, stole, and cope, ascended the predella and seated himself on a faldstool. Francis, Caesar, and Ponziano, knelt before him. From the ceremonial book he chanted the opening prayer: "Look kindly, omnipotent and eternal God, upon these Thy servants, who with sincere mind desire to follow Thee. . . . Give unto them the protection of Thy help that no temptation many dissuade them from their purpose. . . ."

Francis had a keen ear for Latin and caught the meaning of the words. He recognized again the suspicion that he might leave. But he smiled contentedly. It was the farthest thing from his mind.

Father Raphael then exhorted the young men to suffer all things cheerfully for Christ, explaining how vast is the treasure of eternal goods which Christ bestows on His true followers. Afterward he blessed the habits.

Francis and his two companions came forward and took off their coats. Father Raphael slipped the black tunic over their heads and fastened a leather belt about their waists. Then he placed a large black cross on the shoulder of each with the words: "Receive, dearest brother, this cross in memory of the cross of our Lord Jesus Christ. Deny thyself under the mighty hand of God, that thou mayest have part with Him in life everlasting."

Next a crown of thorns was placed on the head of each with the words: "Receive, beloved brother, this crown of thorns in memory of the thorny crown of Christ, our Lord. Humble thyself and be subject to everyone for His sake."

Francis knew that this dramatic ritual symbolized the life of self-denial and unworldliness he was to live. Christ Crucified was to be the inspiration of his life, the model of his conduct, and the principal object of his affections.

The young men now knelt to receive their new names indicating admission to a new family, each wondering what name the master would bestow upon him.

"Caesar Calandrelli," Father Raphael began, "you will henceforth be known as Confrater Philip of the Sorrowful Virgin. Ponziano Gismondi, you will be known as Confrater Hermenegild of the Heart of Jesus. . . .

"Francis Possenti," Father Raphael continued, "you will henceforth be known as Confrater Gabriel of the Sorrowful Virgin."

Francis smiled. "Not a bad name . . . not bad at all," he thought.

The title "confrater," a Latin word meaning "associate brother," is applied to all clerical novices and students in the Passionist Congregation to distinguish them from the "fraters" or lay brothers. The name Gabriel was in honor of the archangel who brought the news to Mary that she was to be the Mother of God, and the title was that of her

Sorrows. Even if Francis had been left to pick a name for himself, he felt he could hardly have found a better one.

The vesting ceremony concluded with Benediction, and the rest of the day was kept as a holiday. Father John Baptist was the only relative of Gabriel who attended the ceremony. Afterward he congratulated his nephew and joined with him in the community celebration.

Alone in his room that evening Gabriel wrote to his father: "The long desired day has come at last. . . . Today I put on with unutterable joy the holy religious habit and took the name of Confrater Gabriel of the Sorrowful Virgin. Up to now I have not had the least shadow of a difficulty either as regards the religious life or my vocation. . . ."

Sante's heart sank. Those words didn't sound as if his son would be returning soon. The rest of the letter was taken up with a request for forgiveness for past faults and recommendations to his brothers.

Signor Possenti was still not satisfied that his son was equal to the strenuous obligations of the Passionist life. He mulled over his thoughts for several days, then put them in writing. Gabriel received the letter about the middle of October.

A week later he replied to his father: "The peace and joy I feel here far surpass what I experienced at home. Be quite certain of this, dear Papa, and believe the word of your son who speaks to you from a full heart. I would not exchange a quarter of an hour in this place for a year amid the glitter and enjoyment of the world!"

After this emphatic rejection of any suggestion that he return, Gabriel became more familiar and explained why he could not write more frequently. "It is not the custom

to write so often," he said. "But Father Master has assured me that he will give me permission to write if I
become ill, or if I have something particular to tell you.
For the rest, do not become uneasy. I am very well, and
I shall not fail to write when there is need. . . ."

In the letter he added a postscript for his brothers,
Michael and Vincent, warning them against the reading
of romantic novels, which at home, had filled his mind
with distractions. He then described the celebration of the
Feast of Paul of the Cross, and ended with greetings
to a long list of friends and acquaintances in Spoleto.

Gabriel, however, did not tell his father that part of
his daily work in the monastery now consisted in mopping
the novitiate washroom and dusting the recreation room.
Nor did he mention the fact that the master was beginning
to mortify his high spirits with rebukes, sometimes deliberately embarrassing him in front of his companions. He felt
these humiliations deeply. Often the color would rush to
his cheeks and his eyes would flash. But then just as
quickly he would control his temper and kneel to ask
pardon for his fault.

Sometimes Gabriel was asked to do things that were
almost beyond his ability; then he was blamed for not
accomplishing them. When he showed discouragement or
resentment, he was humiliated all the more. He knew this
was necessary to develop in him the virtues of obedience
and humility.

In such training Father Raphael was only following the
Rule of St. Paul of the Cross. "Let the novices," it directs,
"serve in the kitchen, sweep the house, and give other
proofs of Christian submission and patience. For this purpose, too, they shall be publicly reprehended, particularly

in the refectory, and shall sometimes eat sitting on the floor, and shall perform other acts of humility and mortification ordered by the superiors, from which it may be clearly known whether they have a real love of being despised; whether they are dead to themselves and to the world, in order to live only for God, in God, and through God, willingly hiding their life in Christ, who for our sake chose to become the reproach of men and the outcast of the people, giving the most faultless example of all virtues."

From first to last Paul of the Cross insisted that his subjects be actuated always by the example of Christ who humbled Himself even to the death of the cross. His constant reminder to them was: "Remember that one grain of pride is sufficient to overthrow a mountain of holiness. God reveals His sublime secrets only to those who are humble of heart. Therefore, entertain a sincere contempt of yourself, and let it be your greatest desire to be regarded as an object worthy of contempt."

Confrater Gabriel took the rule to his heart. He meditated upon the significance and necessity of humility in his spiritual life, and then set about practicing that virtue in little ways. Whenever he was late for an assignment or accidentally broke something he was using, he would go immediately to the master's room and ask for a penance. When the laundry was ready for distribution, he deliberately picked out the torn articles for himself and left the good ones for others. In the refectory he tried to select the poorest piece of fruit or cut off for himself the hard end of the cheese.

Sometimes, though, he didn't succeed in his efforts to cultivate humility. Then he made the very faults into which he slipped just so many stepping-stones toward that

perfection for which he yearned. One day in recreation
he was irritated by a remark of a companion. Turning on
the offending novice, he blurted, "You can tell an ass by
his braying!"

He later begged pardon of the young man and wrote
a resolution in his notebook: "I will try never to provoke
anyone by using sharp words, nor will I speak in such
a manner as to make anyone feel bad. My answers will
always be mild, my manners agreeable."

Not only did Gabriel have trouble with himself, his
companions and the master, but he also had to reckon
with the rigidity of Father Norbert. As vice-master this
priest had the responsibility of supervising the external
work of the novices, so he was constantly checking on
their activities in the sacristy, the kitchen, and the garden.
As far as he was concerned, there were only two ways
of doing things — his way and the wrong way. Gabriel
often saw better ways of doing things, but whenever he
tried to improve his work, he was called to task.

Finally he complained to Father Raphael. "I can't seem
to please the vice-master!" he exclaimed. "If I try to do
something better than the others, he gives me a penance
. . . or makes me do it over."

"Remember, Confrater," the master said kindly, "it is
the spirit that counts. The spirit in which you do a thing
is far more important than what you accomplish. God
does not need you. In one instant with His divine power
He can accomplish more than you can achieve in a whole
lifetime. But He sees fit to take your poor efforts as the
measure of your love for Him. It is not so much *what*
you do, as the reason *why*."

These words made a deep impression on Gabriel. When

he returned to his cell he took out his notebook and wrote at the head of all his other resolutions: "I will attempt day by day to break my will into little pieces. I want to do God's holy will, not my own!"

Day by day he was learning that there was a great deal more to becoming a Passionist than he first imagined. It was one thing to adjust to the external discipline, but quite another to get the Passionist spirit.

But Gabriel's time was not completely taken up with humiliations, privations, and penances. Every Thursday and Sunday afternoon the novices had time off for hikes in the surrounding countryside. Sometimes they went down to the nearby Chienti River to fish. At other times, especially on festivals when the recreation periods were longer, they went off into the hills for a picnic. These outings he enjoyed immensely. The only thing he missed was his gun.

On one of the walks through the neighborhood he was telling Father Raphael how he used to make snares for rabbits and what fine catches he sometimes made.

"Why don't you try that here?" the master asked.

Gabriel was delighted. "That is an easy obedience, Your Reverence!" Accordingly, the project that afternoon was the making and setting of traps.

For Christmas that year his brothers sent him a number of novels. They had forgotten his warning about such works and remembered only that he had enjoyed them so much at home.

Gabriel gave the books to Father Raphael and asked him to dispose of them. In his next letter to his father, he commented: "Thank Michael and Vincent for those books, but please remind them that such reading is no longer useful to me."

During the holiday season he was surprised to receive a visit from his sister Teresa and her husband Pellegrino Pellegrini. They traveled from their home in Terni a few miles to the south to spend an afternoon with him. To her he was the same affectionate Checchino she had always known, and she was pleased to see that his health was holding up. In a subsequent letter to her brother she thanked him for his hospitality and told him how much she enjoyed her visit. In fact, she thought she would come back again at Easter.

This announcement upset Gabriel. He loved his sister very much and would have been delighted to see her often. But the novitiate was not the place to be cultivating human attachments. Not wanting to hurt his sister's feelings by telling her himself, he asked his father to dissuade her from this trip.

"As you know," he wrote March 8, 1857, "Teta has informed me that after Easter she will come with Pellegrino to visit me. I leave it to you to consider if a brother should not be overjoyed at receiving relatives who are so affectionate. But in anticipating such a visit, I feel that it would be a great source of distraction to me. Accordingly, I want you to avert it. Try to postpone it to some future date, when I shall have finished my novitiate. It might be on the occasion of a visit that I have promised to pay my aunt, Sister Maria Teresa, after my novitiate.

"Dearest Papa," he continued, "knowing how ardently you desire my eternal salvation, I have not the slightest doubt that you will explain clearly to them what I have told you. I have, in fact, resolved to avoid any such distractions during my novitiate, and I am positively determined to keep this resolution, as far as I am concerned,

even at the risk of being impolite. You must not be surprised at this resolution. I know my own weakness, and
while I fall daily into many faults, I still wish to remove
from the enemy every possible occasion, even remote ones,
of tempting me into other faults.

"Do not imagine either," he added, "that this decision
has been imposed on me, or even hinted at, by my superiors. They would probably be quite indifferent to these
visits and would put no obstacle in their way. It comes
solely from my own weakness which obliges me resolutely
to avoid everything that would give the devil the least
hold on me."

More and more Gabriel desired to possess God, and
with his impetuous nature he was ready to do anything
to achieve that end. He had relinquished the things of
this world and now wanted to give his heart exclusively
to God. Any attachment of family or friends that might
in any way draw him away from this purpose had to be
broken.

"I am afraid," he explained to Father Raphael, "that
my natural affection for my family is a hindrance to the
love of God. That is why I want to check it."

A similar fear induced him to pass up a short trip with
his fellow religious to the nearby town of Civitanova to
see Pope Pius IX. After Gabriel entered the novitiate, the
political situation had taken a turn for the worse. The
Republic of Piedmont was openly agitating for a United
Italy and trying to lure the people from loyalty to the
Holy Father. Pius decided, therefore, to make a good will
tour of his domain. On May 19 he was due to arrive in
Civitanova just six miles away, and most of the community

from Morrovale were on hand to welcome him. Gabriel deliberately denied himself this pleasure.

In all this, however, there was no feeling of martyrdom. "My life is one of unending joy," he said in a letter to his father just four days later. "The days, the very months, seem to fly by. I am really most happy serving our divine Lord and our Lady, who daily reward their servants with so much generosity. . . . Now I understand those words which I heard so often and which at the time seemed quite commonplace and without much meaning. 'He who enters religion, chooses the better part.'"

In July, when the Italian sun beat down hottest on the monastery, Gabriel began to know real discomfort. His heavy habit weighed upon him and sometimes the heat was almost suffocating. No matter where he happened to be, indoors or out, everything he had on was soaked with perspiration. Crickets sizzled around the cloister courtyard and the monastery seemed to be a gigantic frying pan.

As though this heat was not enough penance, Gabriel asked Father Raphael for permission to wear the *catenella* in preparation for the day of his religious profession. This instrument was an uncomfortable metal chain worn about the waist under the clothing. The master denied the request. A little later, thinking that he might have changed his mind about the matter, Gabriel asked again.

"All right," the master replied, "but you must wear it outside your habit! Let the others see what a glutton you are for penance."

Gabriel blushed. That was certainly not what he wanted. But he conquered his embarrassment and, as Father Raphael had directed, wore it outside his habit for the rest of the day. That night he was happy to discard it.

Even yet Sante Possenti was not convinced that the Passionist life was the one for his son. He wrote to his brother-in-law, the Capuchin Father John Baptist, and asked him to interview Francis once more. This the priest did in the presence of Father Raphael. If this final cross-examination exasperated Gabriel, he gave no sign of it. He certainly convinced his uncle of his sincerity and the master was more than satisfied with him.

In his last letter written as a novice, Gabriel pleaded with his father to be reasonable and attend his profession of vows. "I well remember," he wrote, "the promise that I made you to return home if I found that I was not called by our Lord to this religious congregation. But how, dearest father, can I leave so loving a Master as Jesus Christ and a Mother so full of tenderness as Mary? The more pain I give to their Sacred Hearts . . . the more they teach me that they alone are the dispensers of true joy and happiness. I do not deserve so great a favor. I am indeed unworthy of it. God knows it is my heart that speaks.

"I look forward with the greatest eagerness to seeing you on the day of my profession, which, God willing, will take place on September 22."

Gabriel continued on with assurances of prayers for all the family and asked a final favor of his father, that he send ten crowns to the Father Guardian of the Franciscan monastery on Monte Luco for a novena of Masses.

"I made a solemn promise to the Blessed Virgin Mary," he said, "to do something for the souls in purgatory if she would see me through to the beautiful and longed-for day of my holy profession. . . . I am perfectly sure that you will be kind enough to carry out this last wish of mine. I have so often had proof of the readiness with which you tried to please both my brothers and myself in everything, that I have not the least doubt that you will all the more readily grant me this favor. Accordingly I thank you in anticipation."

Sante sent the requested money to the Father Guardian, but refused to attend his son's profession.

CHAPTER VI

A CHANGED CHECCHINO

"If any man make a vow to the Lord, or bind himself by an oath, he shall not make his word void, but shall fulfill all that he promised." (Num. 30:3.)

The long struggle against the opposition of his family, to become a Passionist was now ending. Gabriel Francis Possenti prostrated himself on the floor of the sanctuary in the Church of Our Lady of the Oaks at Morrovale. Beside him lay his companion, Hermenegild Gismondi. Their classmate, Caesar Calandrelli, was no longer with them. Three months earlier he had been judged unsuited for the religious life and had returned to Spoleto.

Father Norbert, deacon for the ceremony of profession, began the reading of the Passion of our Lord according to St. John. In a few moments the two youths would rise and kneel before Father Raphael to profess their vows for life.

Gabriel realized that once he pronounced those words he broke forever the ties of home and family. There was no turning back after that. But there was no fear in him, only confidence and a quiet joy. With God's help he could bear any trial or trouble that might come his way. The future had no terrors for him. He was confident he was where he belonged.

At the words, *emisit spiritum*, indicating the death of Christ, Father Norbert stopped. Gabriel and Hermenegild rose, and each in turn pronounced his vows as a Passionist.

Gabriel would have liked the whole world to witness his profession, but of his relatives only his uncle, Father John Baptist, was present. A group of his friends, including Peter Parenzi and Philip Giovannetti, had planned to come for the ceremony. But it would have been embarrassing for them to make the trip when his father and family had refused. Instead they sent their regrets.

When each had pronounced his formula of vows, Father Raphael responded in the name of the Church: "I, on the part of God, promise you eternal life, if you faithfully observe these vows."

A thrill ran through Gabriel. "In no other ceremonial," he thought, "is this marvelous promise made. It is not in the marriage ritual, nor in the ordination of a priest. There is nothing like it even in the consecration of a bishop. If only I keep my vows, I have the Church's guarantee of salvation."

Father Raphael then fastened the distinctive Passionist emblem on the left side of Gabriel's habit and mantle, saying: "Receive, beloved brother, this sacred Sign as the victorious standard of your profession, and beneath it fight the good fight by living fastened to the cross of Jesus Christ."

After the ceremony everyone went into the garden to congratulate the newly professed. The rector, radiating a quiet charm and graciousness, moved among the guests and religious. Gabriel sat a little apart with his uncle, and the two reminisced about all that had happened since a similar celebration the year before.

"The big news," Gabriel told his uncle, "is that I am going to remain here with Father Bernard Mary, Vincent, and Hermenegild, until the newcomers, Michael and Charles, are professed. The provincial has decided to hold us at the novitiate until there are enough to form a new class. Then we will go to Pieve Torino to begin our formal studies for the priesthood."

"Will you continue with the novices?"

"Oh, no!" Gabriel replied. "We'll live with the other professed and have our own director, Father Norbert."

The Capuchin was curious. It sounded like a makeshift arrangement. "What are you going to do," he asked, "while you wait for these other students?"

"Study Latin and Greek."

"But I thought you had finished your classical training at college. Father Aloysius told me you had the best grades in your class for both Latin and Greek and that you won the highest awards the Jesuits could give."

"But I can always learn more."

"From whom?"

"Father Norbert. He is to be our teacher, too."

Father John Baptist smiled quizzically, and Gabriel knew he should change the subject. Father Norbert had no special training and like so many self-taught persons he did not recognize his own limitations. He was ready to undertake the instruction of this new group, knowing less about the subjects than his pupils did.

During their review that fall it became immediately

obvious that there were many things about both languages that Father Norbert did not know. But when Confrater Gabriel, who was the most accomplished of the class, ventured to correct him, he received a penance for his trouble. It was very trying.

Even more distressing was the fact that Gabriel was becoming bored at prayer and meditation. All his former fervor seemed to vanish. His spirit was dry and barren, and he had to force himself to keep his mind on what he was doing. Even his ardent desire for perfection was gone, and temptations against purity began to assail him. He turned to Father Norbert for help, but there was little relief.

One day in private conference he blurted out: "I'm almost afraid to tell you this, Your Reverence. I have temptations against God. It seems to me that God is cruel. How can He make me so miserable when I am trying to serve Him?"

"God does not send those temptations to you," the director explained. "He only permits them. Such trials will lead you to a loftier faith, a firmer hope, and a purer love."

By Christmastime the temptations had abated. When Gabriel wrote to his father on December 20, he was once more joyful and commented on the lights he had received in prayer. "I am overjoyed that the darkness that enveloped my spirit — the blindness I had — has now vanished through the goodness of Jesus and Mary."

In gratitude for this special grace Gabriel wanted to show his appreciation by some special offering or gift of himself. While reflecting on the matter he came across a pamphlet by Father Gaspar Olider, entitled "The Heroic Act." In the treatise this Theatine priest recommended that devotees of Mary offer through her hands to God all of the satisfactory merit of their good works during life and all of their suffrages after death for the souls in purgatory. The idea appealed to Gabriel and he asked permission to make this offering. Father Norbert approved.

In the Christmas mail there was a letter from Michael in which his brother expressed dissatisfaction with his medical studies and gave a hint that he might like to join the Passionists. "Are you really content, Checchino?" he asked. "Tell me about your life and the horarium you follow."

The news was almost too good to be true. How he would love to have his older brother with him! For several days he prayed and reflected on the best answer to send. Then on New Year's day he began a long letter to Michael.

"Dear brother," he wrote, "I want to open my heart to you, as one should to a brother. But what can I say? I do not want to upset you, but those questions of yours have made a profound impression upon me. I have not ceased from the moment I read them to pray for you in a particular way. . . .

"Dear Michael, will, perhaps, that happy and blessed hour come to you as it came to me, even though I am more unworthy than you? Do you not believe that she who is called the Refuge of Sinners will turn her merciful eyes upon you? I hope so, and if it be so, I can think of nothing better to say, than 'Arise, and come!'

"Do not follow my example! Although called by our Lord I went on from day to day procrastinating. No! If you have a vocation, do not hesitate for an instant. Cast behind you your dreams of a career, relatives, and worldly attachments, and put your hand to the work. Do not allow the devil to flatter you with promises. Begin at once to follow Jesus! If I had waited another moment, I would probably not have found myself where I am now.

"Have recourse to Mary, and if she has obtained such graces for you, recompense her in some manner by placing at her feet the sacrifice of everything, telling her — and please don't forget this — *I give all to you: knowledge, relatives, possessions.*

"If I am to have the happiness of seeing you with me," he continued, "write at once. I shall then arrange everything with our provincial. If, however, I deceive myself, act as if I have not written you. This is what I feel in my heart. Therefore, I hope you will take it in good part. . . ."

Gabriel then launched into a long explanation of the Passionist life with a detailed account of the daily schedule. He mailed the letter and waited anxiously for Michael's reply. But no answer came. The older Possenti let the matter go. As his brother had promised, his silence was taken as an indication that Gabriel was wrong. He never again mentioned the matter.

By January of 1858 Sante Possenti had completed sixteen years as the grand assessor at the supreme court in Spoleto. For some time he had been thinking of retiring, and finally decided to do it. He was sixty-nine years old and in failing health. Gabriel encouraged his father to put down the burdens of office and recommended that he purchase a villa in the country, or make his home in Rome, where Michael was studying. A month later Sante did retire, but he stayed on at Spoleto.

When Gabriel learned that his father had finally taken the step, he warmly approved the decision. "My very dear father," he wrote, "I thank God for having arranged your retirement. The less you have of the turmoil of the world, the more you can bend your efforts to prepare for your last end. . . ."

In the same letter he mentioned that he was going to Fermo with Father Norbert to see a doctor. He had been bothered with headaches, and the provincial recommended a complete checkup. While there he planned to visit his sister Teresa.

When the two Passionists stopped at the Pellegrini home, Teresa was dismayed to observe that her brother was so thin and pale. "You seem lost in the folds of your habit!" she exclaimed.

Gabriel laughed at her remark. "I guess you can criticize, Teta," he teased in turn, "for you'd make two of me!"

He was especially delighted to meet his little nephews and niece. Then almost immediately he asked, "Are they consecrated to our Blessed Mother?"

"No — what do you mean?"

"Every child," he explained, "should be dedicated to our heavenly Mother. I hope you will make the consecration of them very soon."

Teresa noticed a new charm seemed to radiate from her brother and he fascinated her in a way he had never done before. She was worried about his health, but convinced he was where he belonged.

After about an hour Gabriel suggested to Father Norbert that they leave. The director simply shrugged his shoulders. "In this house," he smiled, "your sister is superior. You can't leave until she tells you!"

During the rest of the day, every time he hinted at leaving, Teresa reminded Gabriel about the previous Easter visit she had planned. He entered into the spirit of her teasing and enjoyed himself immensely. Finally, after dinner, he and Father Norbert went over to the Jesuit house, where they spent the night.

The doctor's report showed nothing wrong, and Gabriel immediately sent the good news to his father. These were days of frequent letters between the old man and his son. Father Norbert knew about conditions at home and how Sante had opposed his boy's going to the Passionists. Feeling that Confrater Gabriel's letters might do some good, he gave him permission to write whenever he wished.

Sometimes Gabriel became a little uneasy about so much correspondence. On May 27 he commented: "I write you with a little scruple, since I am the only one who writes so frequently. . . . But I write, in part, to relieve you of any anxiety. If I were to delay my letters, I feel I would be guilty of an omission."

Every question his father asked was promptly answered. If advice was asked, he gave it. When he gave an exhortation, it was generally prefaced by the words "with my heart on my lips." He had come across that expression in the writings of St. Paul of the Cross, and finding it very expressive, he made it his own.

At the beginning of summer, word reached Morrovale of the death from tuberculosis of one of the students at the monastery of the Immaculate Conception in Isola Gran Sasso. He was Confrater Peter of the Most Holy Virgin. His family lived at Morrovale, so the fathers there held a solemn Requiem in suffrage for him and invited his relatives.

The rector preached an eloquent sermon, assuring his

listeners that Peter was in heaven. Gabriel felt a twinge of envy. "How fortunate," he thought, "to die in a slow, wakeful consumption, in a love that offers all!"

He went alone to the chapel and knelt before the altar. "Dear Jesus," he pleaded, "grant that I may die young — just like Peter."

When Father Norbert learned of this prayer, he was aghast. "Don't ever make such an imprudent prayer again!" he warned. "I absolutely forbid it!"

In July a chapter was held to elect new superiors. Father Basil of the Crucified became provincial and one of his first acts was to reappoint Father Norbert as director and professor of Gabriel's class. He also instructed the little group to transfer immediately to Pieve Torino and begin their formal studies for the priesthood.

Gabriel paid a farewell visit to his uncle, Father John Baptist. Then with Father Norbert and his companions he set out on foot for the Retreat of St. Augustine, nearly forty-five miles due west of Morrovale in the valley of the Chienti River. Fortunately they had very little luggage to carry, for most of their things had been sent ahead in a wagon. Each had only a knapsack with lunch and a few incidentals.

The evening of the first day they stopped in Tolentino at the monastery of the Franciscan Fathers. The friendly friars gave them a hot meal and lodging for the night. Then after a short visit to the tomb of St. Nicholas, they headed into the lower Apennines for the last lap of their journey.

The sky had become overcast as they made their way into the mountains, and heavy, lead-colored drops slanted through the air to lash their faces. They broke against their noses and cheeks, exploding with a splash, as if they were hollow and full of air. What annoyance they caused, Francis offered up for the souls in purgatory as he trudged along with his companions.

As they came within sight of the retreat, situated just south of the town of Pieve Torino on a swampy plateau where the Chienti River turns back on itself, Gabriel's heart sank. All he could see was a quadrangular shaped building with a little church adjoining. "What a miserable place," he thought. "And we have to call it *home!*"

After meeting the community and taking supper, Gabriel was shown to his room on the second floor, a room with an outside, south exposure. He was glad he had this outside exposure, rather than one of the rooms that faced on the tiny courtyard, which gave him a view of the river and the mountains beyond.

Later, thinking that he had fared better than Hermenegild, whose room was on the inside, facing the courtyard, he offered to change. Father Norbert, misinterpreting the motive that prompted this suggestion, commented curtly, "Be content with what you have! None of us is satisfied with our quarters here, but we're not complaining!"

The first few days at Pieve Torino were spent in whitewashing the rooms and making preparations for the school year. In a letter to his father on August 2, Gabriel described the trip to Pieve Torino and asked for his notebooks in philosophy. He omitted all comment about the place itself.

The humidity of the swampy lowlands soon bothered him. Often at night he would wake up choking. After coughing up phlegm, he would sometimes lie down again and fall asleep. But other times he experienced difficulty getting his breath and would be forced to sit up all night. The next morning he would be quite pale, and dark circles of weariness would ring his eyes. He tried to laugh off these discomforts and not admit how much the sleepless nights bothered him. In December, however, he had an acute attack of bronchitis. His health suddenly collapsed. For two and a half years he had borne up under many kinds of penance and privation. Now he had reached the limit of his physical endurance.

The fasting, discipline, hours of kneeling, going up and down stairs, the heat and cold — all had worn him down. Though he had often been tired, he had never taken a nap. At recreation he had kept a cheerful front. Never had he gone to his director and asked a dispensation.

All had been fine until this transfer to Pieve Torino. Then he began to sense that something was wrong. When going upstairs he had often to pause to catch his breath. Sometimes his knees became so shaky he had to lean against the wall for support. Occasionally he broke out in perspiration for no reason at all. The least little draft affected him, and when he wasn't extremely careful, he caught cold. Most of all, the dampness bothered him. He never seemed warm enough. But when the religious built a fire in the recreation room, he deliberately stayed away from the warmth, trying to mortify himself.

At length one day he fainted from weakness. His companions carried him to bed and summoned the doctor. Father Norbert became so alarmed that he wrote immediately to Sante and asked him to come. But the old man was in poor health himself and unable to travel. By return letter he promised to send his son's old governess Pacifica.

It took Pacifica more than a week to arrange the trip to Pieve Torino. By that time the medicine and rest had checked the bronchial trouble, and Gabriel was able to be up and around. However, he had developed a hard, insistent cough which the physician shrugged off as unimportant. He was satisfied that they had checked the inflammation in the patient's throat and had brought the color back to his cheeks.

When Pacifica arrived at the monastery, Gabriel was still convalescing. As soon as he heard his governess was in the parlor, he hurried down to greet her.

The old lady was startled and pleased by his affectionate embrace and animated chatter. What she didn't realize was that he wanted to forestall any comments about his health. He had to prove that he was as lively and devoted as ever — that life in the monastery hadn't changed him a bit. Pacifica must not suspect that anything was radically wrong with her Checchino. She felt that she owned the Possentis, every one of them, and their troubles were her troubles. Even a hint of sickness or suffering threw her into a turmoil of solicitous concern.

As Pacifica stood in the little monastery parlor, she smiled happily at the young Passionist before her. Her hair was completely white and in her sweet, wrinkled face it was hard to recognize the once stern governess who had been Sante's mainstay, the despair of Francis and his brothers, and the terror of the servants. She was more like a kindly old grandmother, and almost immediately she began fussing with her bag to get out some cookies she had baked especially for this visit.

"They're your favorite kind," she confided. "I have them filled with pecans and honey."

Gabrel made a great deal over the cookies and his compliments brought smiles to Pacifica's face. Then he deftly turned the conversation to the subject of his family and friends.

"Tell me about them," he began. "How is my father . . . Michael . . . Henry . . . and Vincent? Do you ever see Father Aloysius . . . or my old friends, Peter Parenzi and Philip Giovannetti? . . . What are they doing now? . . . Have any of them married?"

Pacifica kept answering questions and reminiscing till the rattle of dishes announced that Brother Peter was preparing dinner in the next room. Father Norbert, before excusing himself, told Gabriel he was to eat with Pacifica. It was an unusual permission and he started to protest.

"That's an obedience!" Father Norbert remarked with a smile. "I want to show your governess that you have learned to obey here better than you did at home."

After dinner the two went outside for a walk in the garden. Gabriel continued to ply Pacifica with questions about affairs at home, and the matter of his recent sickness was forgotten. After two days she was satisfied that Checchino was on the road to recovery and went back to Spoleto to report to Sante in glowing terms of the wonderful reception she had received. And about how happy he was to see her.

In January of 1859 Sante took a turn for the worse. When Gabriel learned that his father was confined to bed, he sent him a tender letter, urging him to find his solace in the truths of Faith. He urged him to read once again what St. Francis de Sales and St. Alphonsus Liguori had to say about suffering. "Their beautiful thoughts," he explained, "will be most consoling to you."

Spring that year was very wet and Gabriel once more took to bed with a touch of bronchitis. After a few days of extra rest and medicine, he was again on his feet. His color, though, was very bad. Father Norbert thought it well to inform Sante again.

This time the old man decided to send his son Michael, who had finished his studies and was practicing medicine in the town of Camerino. When Michael laid eyes on his brother, he was quite alarmed. Gabriel had lost a great deal of weight and had a very suspicious cough. It wasn't good at all.

"Tell me, Checchino," he said, "what do you think of returning home for a few weeks, where we can give you better medical attention? We would all be so happy to have you, and your health would improve much more rapidly."

Gabriel's eyes flashed and he shook his head vehemently: "No, Michael, never! Our Lord has done too much for me in giving me a vocation to this life and so many graces. I couldn't think of leaving."

Michael decided to change the subject. Later he spoke privately with Father Norbert and won from him an assurance that his brother would not have to fast or get up for the night office. Perhaps with these mitigations he would be able to hold on until the class transferred to the Retreat of the Immaculate Conception at Isola Gran Sasso. There he would have the more invigorating mountain air.

CHAPTER VII

THE SAVIOR OF ISOLA

"Thou, O Lord, hast girded me with strength for battle. Thou hast made them that resisted me to bow under me. My enemies Thou hast made to turn their backs to me." (2 Kings 22:40, 41.)

At the end of June Confrater Gabriel and his companions received word from the provincial to leave immediately for the Retreat of the Immaculate Conception at Isola Gran Sasso. This transfer came a month earlier than anticipated, because of a drastic change in the political situation. The whole country was in ferment.

Two months earlier Austria had been forced into war with Piedmont, and almost immediately the Austrians had been soundly beaten at Montebello, Palestro, Solferino, and San Martino. To bolster their position they had withdrawn their troops from the Province of Romagna, soldiers who had been protecting the rights of the Holy See. When this force pulled out, the local authorities were helpless. Revolution spread everywhere. The dissolution of the Papal States had begun.

The safest place in this turmoil seemed to be Isola Gran

Sasso in the Kingdom of Naples. Accordingly, Father Basil ordered the students to move there. It was an almost inaccessible spot in the mountains of Abruzzi, where, surely, they would find peace and tranquillity.

Thus on Monday morning, July 4, 1859, the little band set out for the Retreat of the Immaculate Conception, about ninety-five miles directly south of them. They could not take a direct route, however, for the Apennine range stood in the way. They had to cut over to the Adriatic and go down the coast to Giulianova, then turn inland. Although this made the journey almost twice as far, it afforded them the opportunity of visiting on the way the Passionist monasteries at Recanati, Morrovale, Torre San Patrizio, and Giulianova.

By the time they reached the last monastery, named after the Annunciation, Gabriel was so exhausted that he had to go to bed immediately. But the next day he felt much better and was delighted to see a companion of novitiate days, Brother Sylvester, who was now cook for the community. Brother Sylvester proudly showed Gabriel all the improvements he had made in the kitchen.

One thing that especially caught Gabriel's eye was a statue of the Blessed Virgin, which Sylvester had painted and set in a little shrine. "It is quite beautiful!" he exclaimed. "I never realized you were such an artist. I like especially that delicate smile."

Gabriel reached for the statue and lifted it from its pedestal. As Brother Sylvester watched, he held it for a moment in his hands, examining it closely. Then impulsively he kissed it. It was the action of a moment. He blushed and put it back.

Next morning the group set off on the final stage of

their journey. The rector had arranged for a carriage to take them the twenty-five miles from Giulianova to Montorio al Vomano, where the road ended. After lunch at the Capuchin monastery, they hired mules for the ride up the steep trail to Isola Gran Sasso.

The name means literally the *Isle of the Great Rock.* The town is situated on a high plateau and surrounded almost entirely by two narrow rivers, the Temperino and the Mavone, which flow down from the snows above and wind themselves around the slopes. Mountains ring the place about, forming a giant amphitheater, and overshadowing everything is one tremendous peak, a naked mass of granite that rises 9615 feet above sea level.

Gran Sasso or the *Great Rock of Italy* is the highest point of the Apennines. Around its giant base stretch broad pasture lands, studded here and there with olive groves and vineyards. Forests of dark firs and green birches climb up its sides, until the barren granite forbids their closer approach. Then for hundreds of feet the great rock towers in a line almost perpendicular, its face smoothed and polished by the winds and rains of unnumbered centuries.

Sometimes Gran Sasso is wreathed in clouds. At other times it stands like a sharp and brilliant cone, its summit glistening in the sunlight with a crown of snow. Serene in its exalted height it looks down on all the lesser peaks and on the little Monastery of the Immaculate Conception, set on the east end of the plateau.

The long journey from Pieve Torino had taken more out of Gabriel than either he or Father Norbert realized. If they had not hired mules for the steep climb to Isola, he would never have made it. As it was, he kept slipping off his mount. The others joked with him about not knowing how to ride. He smiled weakly and prayed desperately for strength to hang on.

Finally at a promontory called Devil's Finger, they came in sight of the monastery on the other side of a steep ravine. Beyond was the little town of Isola with its seven hundred and sixty-eight inhabitants.

"Magnificent!" Gabriel exclaimed. "I've never seen any place like it."

All agreed that its beauty had no rival and hurried on to their new home, where they were welcomed by the community and given supper.

The monastery was built in the form of a rectangle, with the church jutting off from the front. Gabriel's room was on the inside, looking out into a little stone-covered court-yard. It had a view of nothing, and even the sight of the mountains round about was blocked by overhanging eaves. But he didn't mind.

All Gabriel wanted was some rest. He felt weaker than he had ever felt before . . . and slowly he lay back on the bed. There was suddenly an unusual pain in his chest and then the sensation of something warm and sweet in his mouth. He sat up in fright and held a handkerchief to his lips. It came away red.

For a moment he did not know what to do. Should he tell Father Norbert? But what good would that do? Maybe he was going to die! But that was hardly likely after just a little hemorrhage.

He decided to wait till morning and went quietly to sleep. After he got up at six o'clock, he assisted at Prime and made his hour of prayer with Mass and Holy Communion. Then he went to tell his superior. He felt no pain, no ill effects. Father Norbert was quite disturbed, but he finally decided they should wait to see if there would be a second hemorrhage. After all, the air and mild climate would surely help his condition.

A week later Gabriel was feeling much better. Color had come back into his cheeks and his cough was much improved. He decided to write his father.

"Dearest father in Jesus Christ," he began, using a more religious title than he had ever invoked before. "A week ago Sunday evening we arrived happily at this retreat. The many fruit trees about the place prove that it has a very mild climate. Thanks to heaven, I am very pleased with it. The prolonged journey here and the wish to be able to tell you how to address your letters to me accounts for the fact I haven't written sooner."

He then told his father of the best way to send mail and warned that his own letters might not be so frequent. It was not that his love was diminishing, but rather that deliveries in Isola were often delayed and that his time was now more occupied.

"Do not think for a moment," he asserted, "that I ever forget you or my other relatives. Sometimes people stupidly say that a son, after becoming a religious, no longer remembers what his parents have done and the affection they have given. That is not so! Believe me, dear papa, my love for you is only perfected here in the monastery and I am constantly reminded of the benefits I have received."

Father Norbert added a long postscript to this letter, mentioning that in the past three years he had been obliged several times to restrain Confrater Gabriel from penances that would have been injurious to his health. "He has always been docile to my direction," he assured Sante, "but his health of late has been poor, for which I fear that the air of Pieve Torino was to blame. . . . I myself have suffered from the same trouble. But the air here is invigorating, and in the nine days we have enjoyed it, we have all improved. Your son, especially, is looking better and I hope he will soon be completely recovered."

In order that Gabriel might benefit as much as possible from the fresh air and sunshine, Father Norbert put him in charge of the flower garden. Gabriel joyfully set to work on a special plot on the west side of the monastery, which he named the Little Garden of the Madonna.

Here he could be found almost every day during free time, digging and spading, watering and trimming; and soon, enough blooms appeared to make some bouquets for the altar.

When the frosts threatened in the fall, he dug up the plants and put them in a greenhouse he had made in the courtyard. He also kept a number of potted ferns there, which were brought out to decorate the altar on feast days.

One day when the students were cleaning a storeroom, they found an old statue of the Blessed Virgin, which was chipped and discolored. Gabriel went immediately to Father Norbert and asked if he could redecorate it.

"Fine!" the director said, "but do you think you can do it?"

"I'd like to try, Your Reverence," he replied.

For many days he worked on the statue, which was about four feet high. First he repaired the chips and cracks with plaster and then blended paints till gradually the hands and face took on a lifelike hue. But the painted garments made the whole thing appear dull. Then he conceived the idea of making a gown for it. In the tailor shop there was some dark green velvet material left over from a set of vestments. With it he designed, cut, and sewed a neatly pleated gown with a fancy lace collar. Over the Madonna's hair he draped a long veil, trimmed with lace, which flowed into a cope that reached to her ankles. In her left hand, held limply, was a white muff, studded with pearls. The heart of the Virgin was pierced with a sword and Gabriel cleverly stained the cloth around the wound to give the appearance of blood.

When he finished, the statue was an object of beauty and inspiration. Father Valentine, the rector, was so pleased that he had a special niche prepared for it over the tabernacle in the monastery chapel. Gabriel was delighted to see *his* Madonna so honored.

These were days filled with study. He was particularly interested in any theological reference to the Mother of God, and when he came across some striking truth about her in the writings of the Fathers of the Church, he copied it in his notebook. From these quotations he composed what he called his *Simbolo Mariano*. It was made up of fifty-two propositions regarding Mary and covered nineteen pages of fine, careful script. He recited it often to remind himself of the privileges and prerogatives of his heavenly Mother.

His devotion to Mary was becoming more and more intense. Father Norbert was taken aback when he came in one day and asked permission to burn or carve her name over his heart.

"Good heavens, Confrater! I could never permit anything like that!"

Gabriel was persistent. Finally, to satisfy him the director said, "You may paint her name there, but nothing more!"

With a similar persistence he obtained permission to abstain from fruit for forty days preceding the Feast of the Assumption. He called this "Mary's Lent." It was quite a privation, for fruit was then in season and the religious used it as an important part of their diet.

From the days of his novitiate Gabriel had also been asking his superiors for permission to make a vow, offering everything to Jesus through Mary's hands, imitating her virtues in his daily life, and spreading devotion to her by word and example. The master of novices would not even hear of such a thing, and Father Norbert, too, put him off repeatedly. Now, as the Feast of Our Lady of Sorrows approached, the director gave in.

On the morning of the third anniversary of his profession Gabriel knelt before Father Norbert in the monastery chapel and made his vow privately. It was the culmination of his most ardent desires and the beginning of a yet more intense love for the Mother of Sorrows.

Gabriel had always been a conscientious student, but he now redoubled his efforts. The subject matter of his present studies was much more interesting, and he knew that the more proficiency he obtained, the better he would be able to help souls. Moreover, increased knowledge of God and the spiritual life would help his own spiritual growth.

In order not to lose a moment of the time allotted to study, he made a resolution never to leave his room during these periods unless called by obedience. On his desk he had a little reminder of this and on his door he tacked a card which warned: *"Don't Leave This Cell!"* It made him pause and reflect each time he left as to whether his absence was necessary.

In a letter to his brother Henry, who was now studying at the Seminary in Spoleto, he exclaimed: "Shun idleness and apply yourself diligently to study! One of the thoughts that frightens me when I think of becoming a priest is the study it demands. There are indeed very few days in which this thought does not give me serious concern."

Another thing that concerned him was the political situation. But it was not a personal concern. When his father expressed his worries about possible danger, Gabriel reassured him with the words: "This place where I am now is the safest possible. It is so far from all the important towns that we are not likely to see any of the war."

When the matter came up in recreation Gabriel would try to turn the discussion to other subjects. "All this talk about riots and battles," he exclaimed, "is not for us. Let us leave these matters in the hands of God and turn our attention to our studies."

Meanwhile, the war was coming steadily closer. In April of 1859 a revolution had broken out in Sicily and Garibaldi conceived the idea of going to the assistance of the rebels. He had led a force of volunteers victoriously in the Piedmontese service during the campaign against Austria and was anxious for more excitement. With a thousand Piedmontese mercenaries he landed on May 11 at Marsala in Sicily. The Neapolitan troops that tried to resist the landing were so miserably led that they ended up shooting one another. By bluff and audacity, the "Red-Shirts," as Garibaldi called his men, conquered all of Sicily and Naples in three months.

The question then became, "Would Garibaldi proclaim himself head of the Neapolitan Republic and march on

Rome against the Holy Father?" That would bring down the armed fury of all Catholic Europe. The Piedmontese King, Victor Emmanuel, knew that such a move would ruin the chances of a United Italy. Tension was mounting everywhere and insurgents were seizing power in many of the little towns around Isola.

Finally, Victor Emmanuel decided to march south with thirty-five thousand Piedmontese troops and join Garibaldi. The Holy See tried to resist this invasion of its territory, but the Piedmontese on September 18 practically annihilated the papal army at Castelfidardo.

During these days even the peaceful little village of Isola went wild with excitement. Scouts and pillaging parties of the Piedmontese army were getting closer and closer. They were stripping the towns of provisions, confiscating horses and cattle, looting and burning what remained. Wild tales were told of how old men were put to death for resisting these deprivations, of girls being raped, and of little children turned out to starve.

All these terrible things had happened at Orvieto and Perugia. Now the same soldiers were marching on Teramo, Montorio al Vomano, and Aquila. Would they come into the high valley?

A sense of impending calamity seemed to brood over the little town. Men left their fields and huddled together for mutual protection. Then came the frightening rumor that a band of marauders was climbing the trail to Isola. Though they tried not to believe the report, whole families rushed in panic to the mountains. Even some of the Passionists fled.

Father Valentine hid the sacred vessels in the garden well and locked himself in his room. The students were told to take refuge in the church and pray the rosary that Mary might spare the town.

But their prayers were interrupted by the thudding hooves of cavalry. The students knelt in fright, listening. On the horses came — past the church, and down into the town.

What happened in the next hour or so was a nightmare for the poor people who remained at Isola. The soldiers looted and pillaged without opposition. The local militia, hopelessly outnumbered, fled without a fight.

Gabriel was dismayed by the cowardice he saw about him. Rushing to the rector's room he beat on the door. "Your Reverence," he cried, "why don't you stop this looting and plundering? You are pastor of this town and the only authority left. Do something to help your poor people!"

"What can I do?" the rector cried piteously, not even opening the door. "Those men won't listen to me. They are heavily armed . . . and probably drunk! Hide yourself and beg God that they leave us alone!"

All his life the superior had pursued the way of peace. Now with violence all about him the poor man was utterly bewildered. Prudence seemed better than valor. If he could think of nothing else, at least he could hide — and pray.

At the thought of the injustice, anger flared in Gabriel's heart. Fear fell away before its fury. "Can I help them?" he shouted.

"Do anything you want!" the rector replied in desperation.

Gabriel turned and ran toward the town. On the way he met Xavier Tortella, the hired man, and called to him to follow. About twenty men were ransacking the houses, and here and there could be heard a drunken laugh or the scream of a woman.

He stopped in the middle of the road to let Xavier catch up with him. He saw smoke beginning to billow from one of the houses. "They're trying to fire the place!"

Suddenly a soldier appeared in a doorway. In one hand he held a pistol, with the other he dragged a terrified girl.

Gabriel gaped at the man and watched his face change from harsh tenseness to a half-contemptuous, half ingratiating smile.

"So it's a little monk," he sneered, slipping his pistol back into its holster and moving out into the road until he stood directly in front of Gabriel. "All alone, eh?"

Just then the soldier saw Xavier duck into a doorway. "Who's that following you?"

Gabriel didn't answer. His hand whipped around the soldier's gun butt and snapped the pistol out of its holster. All his training came back to him. He cocked the revolver and pointed it at the startled, bearded face: "Don't move or I'll shoot!"

The soldier released the frightened girl and she darted into the house. Then cupping his hands to his mouth, he shouted for help. Another soldier poked his head out of a nearby door to see what was the matter.

"Drop your gun!" Gabriel shouted, pointing the revolver at him. The startled soldier let his weapon fall and stepped bewilderedly into the street.

Gabriel picked up the second weapon. He was now well armed and a plan of defense formed in his mind. If nothing else, he could show these renegades a sample of his marksmanship. It might scare them, cowards that they were.

"Oh," he thought, "if only the Major could see me now!" But unknown to him, Major O'Reilly was dead. He had fought a brilliant delaying action at Spoleto against the invading Piedmontese. For two weeks he had blocked the greatly superior forces of General Fanti at the end of the Umbrian Valley. But on September 27 he had been killed in a cannonading. That same day the remnants of his little garrison of *La Rocca* had surrendered.

By now the shouts of Gabriel's captives had attracted the attention of the rest of the company and they came running. But seeing the armed Passionist holding two of their comrades at bay, they slowed to a cautious walk. While they were still about ten yards distant, he swung one revolver toward them. "That's far enough!"

A sergeant stepped out in front of the others and surveyed the scene. "What's going on?" he demanded of the captive men.

Gabriel's eyes flashed. Gone was all fear and timidity. "You should know," he snapped. "Put your guns down or I'll be forced to shoot!"

The sergeant laughed. "So one little monk thinks he can stop us, eh?"

Suddenly a lizard darted from the shadows of the house and paused a moment in the road. Gabriel barely took aim as he fired. The kick of the pistol and the acrid smoke of the explosion were sheer delight to the Passionist. The shot was a direct hit and the reptile flipped over on the road.

Dumbfound, the sergeant stared at him, while Gabriel cocked the second revolver and pointed it at the sergeant. "Now order your men to drop their guns!"

The startled officer did as Gabriel demanded and the

soldiers disarmed. Then forcing the frightened man to have
his soldiers empty their pockets and knapsacks, he recovered most of the loot they had collected. And holding
the sergeant at bay he forced them to put out three fires
they had started and to abandon the horses of the company. Finally, he marched the whole company ahead of
him and out of town.

A number of excited townspeople followed at a distance,
their courage taking fire from this fearless student. As the
soldiers took to their heels, someone shouted, "*Viva il
nostro salvatore!*"

"*Viva! . . . Viva!*" they all cried, and in a triumphant procession they accompanied Gabriel back to the monastery.

CHAPTER VIII

"GESU, GIUSEPPE E MARIA"

"Being made perfect in a short space, he
fulfilled a long time."   (Wisd. 4:13.)

Though the war continued around Isola
Gran Sasso, the little town suffered no further raids. No
Piedmontese patrols returned to the valley.

On November 7, 1860, King Victor Emmanuel joined
forces with Garibaldi and the two rode triumphantly into
Naples. Count Cavour, the crafty prime minister of Piedmont, immediately arranged a plebiscite to determine
which of the two leaders the people wanted as their
sovereign. The king won the election. Garibaldi gave up
his command in disgust and retired to the Isle of Caprera.

Victor Emmanuel was now the sole ruler of Italy, except
for Rome and Venice. Nearly every government in Europe
protested his conquest, but there was little they could do.
It was already accomplished.

Mail service was disrupted during this period and
Gabriel's letters to his father practically ceased. On December 4 he was able to send only a very short Christmas
greeting. On December 27 he mailed a longer letter to

his brother Vincent, in which he pleaded: "place yourself in these troubled times with full confidence under the protection of Mary. If she is for you, who can be against you?"

He stressed the same theme again on February 26, when he was able once more to write to his father. Things had been in a bad way at Spoleto since the fall of Fort *La Rocca,* and Sante needed comforting.

"Do you wish, dear father," he wrote, "to live tranquilly in the midst of so many miseries? Do you desire to pass your days in true peace? . . . Then compassionate the Mother of Sorrows by the remembrance of her pains. Read a book which treats of Mary; make the Way of the Cross; recite the Seven Dolor beads and the *Stabat Mater.* Console your heart with Mary; tell her your affairs, your needs. . . ."

When Gabriel brought this letter to Father Norbert for mailing, the director added a postscript, assuring Sante that his son was in fairly good health. "Recently," he noted, "I had to give him a purge for a stomach disorder, but he is normal again. He is contented and happy, but constantly deplores the diversions of his past life, which now fill him with weariness and remorse."

Spring came early that year. The warm, quick rains brought out a froth of blossoms in the orchard. Father Norbert decided to give Gabriel a better room, so he assigned him to one on the west side of the monastery. It afforded much more air and sunlight and gave him a fine view of his garden.

The director also thought he should get more exercise. Accordingly, he sometimes sent him into the fields with the shepherds. At other times he suggested that he catechize the children in the neighboring hamlets of Cesa di

Francia and Pacciano. Gabriel enjoyed those hours with the peasants and they became very fond of him.

Eliseus di Lorenzo was one of the mountaineers who often grazed his flock near the monastery. Gabriel occasionally stopped to visit with him and invariably ended by urging him to say more prayers to the Madonna.

"But I haven't time," the shepherd argued. "I have to keep my eyes on the sheep."

"Nonsense, Eliseus!" Gabriel replied. "You know perfectly well that you don't herd them with your heart. But you can speak with your heart to your heavenly Mother. Maybe if you prayed more, the sheep would act better!"

On May 20 it was arranged that the Passionist students visit the cathedral at Penne to receive minor orders. They traveled by muleback most of the way around the mountain, but it was nonetheless a long and exhausting trip. Gabriel was so spent when they arrived that the director had to help him to bed.

The next morning he was able to participate in the ordination rites. He received tonsure and the four minor orders from Bishop Vincent d'Alfonso. It was then arranged that the class return during the Ember days in September for the subdiaconate.

On the trip back to Isola, Gabriel was riding with his classmate Michael. Suddenly he reined his mount. His companion glanced at him and saw that his eyes were brimming with tears. "Oh, Michael," he exclaimed, "I feel so many inspirations! God wishes me to be wholly His, but I do not correspond!"

They reached the valley of Isola at dusk. A faint pink still lingered about the summit of Gran Sasso and feathery clouds on the peak were tinged with gold. The stillness of the mountain twilight was all about them as calming as a prayer. "How did I ever manage it?" he wondered. "I've never been so tired."

That night in his room Gabriel had a violent attack of coughing, which racked his weakened body and made him clutch the bed for support. Then came a violent nausea and a gurgling sensation in his throat. He grabbed his handkerchief and put it to his mouth. Suddenly it was filled with blood.

He trembled with delight. His prayer had been heard. Soon he would be with his heavenly Mother. "O my Jesus," he murmured, "I offer You love for love, suffering for suffering, blood for blood. . . ."

When the doctor came, he made out a new prescription. He did not hold out much hope for the recovery of the young man and said so. That evening, when Father Valentine gave his blessing to the community, he recommended Confrater Gabriel to their prayers.

Father Norbert looked in on Gabriel before retiring and urged him to unite his prayers with those of his brethren.

"Why, Your Reverence?" he questioned. "Let me ask rather for a good and holy death. The dangers of offending God are so many."

"No!" the director ordered. "Abandon yourself instead into the hands of God. Let Him decide."

In the days that followed, Gabriel regained some of his strength. He was able to get out of bed, to walk down the corridor, and even to go into the garden. But the mark of death was on him.

One afternoon as Gabriel sat outside enjoying the fresh

air and sunshine, Francis Dionisi, nephew of the provost of Isola, stopped by. The young man whom Gabriel had taught Catechism was home on vacation from medical school at Rome, so he was most solicitous about the health of his friend.

"I'll not live to see you graduate," Gabriel remarked very casually. "My illness is so serious that medicine can offer no remedy. However, I am quite resigned. I even desire to die, for there is nothing in this life that can compare with paradise."

Both his father and governess were also ailing at this time, so he wrote to comfort them. "Patience!" he urged. "Let us all suffer our afflictions for the love of Jesus and Mary, who suffered so much for us. In this way we shall lighten our pains and at the same time not lose the merit to be found in them.

"Last Saturday," he continued a bit wistfully, "I was to have been ordained to the subdiaconate, but that had to be canceled. May the holy will of God be done!"

Actually the war was over and the country should have been at peace. But bands of revolutionaries were still pillaging in the mountain fastnesses between Isola and Penne. Travel there was very dangerous. Father Faustus, the newly-elected provincial did not want to expose the students to such danger. He decided, therefore, to defer the ordinations for a year. At Christmas Gabriel would have received the diaconate and priesthood. Now those hopes were gone.

"I want only the will of God," he said when Father Norbert broke the news.

"My life," he told his director, "is now full of contentment. What more can I enjoy in this vale of tears? I could not be happier than I am. Only my temptations worry me. . . . Sometimes they are terrifying."

At prayer his faith would seem to evaporate into mists that covered his soul. He no longer knew what he wanted or what he believed. In this confusion he would try to turn to Mary and the strengthening remembrance of her power. But the darkness itself only mocked him: "You dream of a lovely Queen and heaven. It is all delusion! Death will lead you to yet deeper night. . . . It will be the night of nothingness."

He seemed to be on the verge of blasphemy. God forgive him! He had not the least consolation from his faith, but every day he did its works. "I have made more acts of faith during the past year," he told his director, "than in all of my past life."

He now believed only by an effort of will, but he did believe. Love actually increased, for these trials instead of turning him away from God, drew him without his realizing it all the closer. And he increased his hope, by repeating over and over again: "God will keep His promises! I know He will!"

In October the superiors called Brother Sylvester from the Retreat at Guilianova and assigned him to take care of Confrater Gabriel. Dizzy spells were becoming more frequent and he suffered violent headaches.

Father Norbert, thinking that perhaps his intense concentration at prayer brought on this condition, forbade Gabriel to make formal meditation. But his interior union with God, which had grown strong again, made his life a continual prayer. He held converse with Him as familiarly as does a child with its father. He sensed the nearness of God as one might sense the presence of a bosom friend, and the joy and delight he experienced in this union were more real and intense than any that had ever come from human attachments.

More and more, too, he realized his own unworthiness. He felt that he was not co-operating with grace as generously as he should. His human weaknesses were keeping him from rendering supreme delight to the One he loved. But what could he do?

One day as Father Norbert was passing his room, Gabriel called him in. "Tell me, Your Reverence," he cried in great agitation, "do you know of anything in my heart, however small, that is not pleasing to God? If you do, tell me, and with His help I will rip it out at any cost."

Gabriel struck and clutched his chest with such violence that the director had to seize his arms. "Stop it!" he ordered. "You'll hurt yourself!"

"Oh, Father," he cried with tears in his eyes, "everything in me must go that is not for God!"

In November Gabriel's health began to fail more rapidly. He could no longer participate in any of the community exercises. He was even unable to kneel up for Holy Communion. One of his companions had to support him.

At night he would fall back utterly exhausted on his bed, yet sleep would not come. One moment he seemed to burn with fever; the next he would be seized with chills.

Some of the townspeople, noticing that he was not in his customary place in church, inquired about him. When they were told of his illness, they immediately brought butter, eggs, cream, and meat. In their need he had protected them. Now whatever they had was his for the asking. A few of the men even pleaded to be admitted to the sickroom.

To Titus Orseni he exclaimed, "All these attentions you good people are offering fill me with confusion. You worry more about me than if I were your king."

On December 19 he wrote his last letter to his father. "Dearest Papa," he began, "I want to remind you that God will not fail to provide for you abundantly, if you are good to Him in the person of His poor. . . . Hear what He says by His prophet: 'Blessed is he who understands concerning the needy and poor; in the evil day the Lord will liberate him and [note this well] make him blessed upon the earth, and will not deliver him into the hands of his enemies.'

"Behold the medicine that liberates from evil, makes one happy upon the earth, safe from his enemies, and consoled on the bed of death. Be liberal with Jesus Christ, and do not content yourself with bestowing upon them a look of pity, hesitating to give them more than a piece of bread. . . .

"Kindly receive the good wishes," he concluded, "which I send you with my heart rather than words. May Jesus, Mary, and Joseph on the coming holy feast render you happy in time and eternity. Don't be concerned if I neglect to write further, for if anything happens, you will be informed."

By Christmas Eve he was so weak he could not go downstairs. They carried him, therefore, to the window in the chapel that looked out on the sanctuary of the church. There he assisted at the solemn ceremonies and there the deacon of the Mass brought him Communion. When he returned to his room, he was so exhausted he could hardly speak.

On December 30, after complete bed rest he felt strong enough to write a letter to his brother Michael. Fittingly, this last message was an eloquent expression of love for Mary.

"Michael," he pleaded, "*Love Mary!* Who is more beautiful, more lovable, more powerful than she? Do not think that, because you cannot see her with your bodily eyes, loving her and speaking with her brings weariness and emptiness. No! Consolations and joys will be all the more pure and filling in that the soul is spiritual and superior to the body.

"Remember, Michael, that people here on earth cannot make you happy. They are inconstant and deceitful in their love. Even if you should find someone without such defects, the one thought of having to separate from that person one day would embitter and torment your heart. But this will never happen to one who chooses Mary. She is lovable, faithful, constant. She will never let herself be outdone in love, but will ever remain supreme. If you are in danger, she will hasten to free you. If you are troubled, she will console you. If you are sick, she will bring you relief. If you are in need, she will help you. She does not look to see what kind of person you have been. She simply comes to a heart that wants to love her. She comes quickly and opens her merciful heart to you, embraces you, consoles you, and serves you. She will even be at hand to accompany you on the trip to eternity."

Repeatedly the pen slipped from his fingers. He knew this would probably be his last greeting to his family, so he asked Michael to show the letter to the others.

"Good-bye, my brother," he said, "and give my love to father and all the family. Assure them, too, that I have always been content here in holy religion. *I would rather by the divine mercy be the least among the Passionists, than be the son of the king and heir to the kingdom!"* He underscored the last sentence.

January of 1862 was a cold, damp month that saw the ground covered with snow and Gabriel growing steadily weaker. Brother Sylvester was kept busy heating bricks and putting them in the bed to warm the patient. A brazier of coals, burning in a corner of the room never quite took the chill off the place. Gabriel, though, was scarcely aware of the cold. He was awaiting death with almost pleasurable anticipation.

"Do you want me to tell you how I feel about leaving this world?" he asked Father Norbert. "I am not the least bit dismayed. Rather I am afraid there is some self-love in the pleasure I experience at the thought."

One of the religious brought him a copy of a periodical, entitled *Science and Faith*. As he thumbed through it, he came across an indulgenced prayer for a happy death. This he carefully copied on a little card and put it on the table beside him. Several times a day he would recite it, each time finding more comfort and interior peace.

As the days wore on, his thin body was more and more racked with pains and his soul went through its Gethsemani of bitterness and desolation. The fever which slowly consumed his vitality left him so prostrate at times that he was unable even to change his position. Frequent coughing spells so irritated his nerves that darts of pain, like sword thrusts, penetrated to every part of his chest and head. His physical depression often reacted upon his spirit, leaving him dejected and melancholy. In this condition the temptations against faith once more assailed him, and it took all the will power he could summon to resist.

His classmates and most of the other religious never

suspected the intensity of his bodily suffering or mental anguish. To them he was always cheerful, always smiling. Each time they visited his room he had a new joke or amusing story to tell.

In February the disease became much worse — constant vomiting, suffocation, loss of consciousness. February 16 he was carried down to church for Sunday Mass. It was the last time he left his bed.

By this time one of the students had to sit up with him each night. The only complaint Gabriel had against the spasms that tore him was that his incessant cough might keep his classmate on edge.

In the morning he would plead with the director to allow the man who had spent the night with him to have a special breakfast and more time for sleep.

Death was inching closer. And he begged for prayers.

On Tuesday afternoon, February 25, he was alone in his room. The infirmarian had gone to participate at Vespers for the Feast of the Solemn Commemoration of the Passion. Suddenly Gabriel tasted blood in his mouth and tried to sit up. But he was too weak. Spasms shook him and a violent hemorrhage occurred. He lay limp and helpless, unable even to cry out.

Fortunately Father Norbert happened to pass the room. He rushed to Gabriel's aid and lifted his head so he would not suffocate. When the infirmarian returned, they decided it was time to anoint him and administer Viaticum.

"I think you are dying, my son," Father Norbert explained.

Gabriel's eyes widened in surprise. For a moment it seemed that the shadow of fear crossed his countenance. Then it was gone and he smiled in acquiescence.

The community was summoned and Father Valentine began the anointing. During the ceremony Gabriel had only one concern, that the rector read the prayers a little louder so he could follow them.

When it came time for the Viaticum, he asked to be clothed in his holy habit, so as to receive his Lord in that religious garb. But it was feared that the rough and heavy garment would be too much for his weakened condition. However, it was placed beside him on the bed.

"I'm so sorry," he murmured as his fingers tenderly caressed the habit. "I wanted to have the consolation of dying in you. . . . Forgive me . . . forgive me. . . ."

When the Blessed Sacrament was brought into his room, he made an effort to rise. Brother Sylvester leaned over and whispered, "Lay back, Confrater. The good Jesus does not wish that." Obediently the patient composed himself and saluted his Eucharistic Lord with the Sign of the Cross.

During the absolution he weakly struck his breast, imploring forgiveness for his offenses. Then his eyes lighted up as the Holy Viaticum was placed on his tongue. As he received the Eucharist, he closed his eyes and folded his hands over his breast.

After the Apostolic Blessing, the patient rallied a bit. It was obvious that he was not going to die immediately, so the religious returned to their appointments. Only Father Norbert remained in the room with him.

"If the Lord wants me tonight," Gabriel murmured, "may His will be done. But I think this illness will be prolonged. In any case, may His will be done!"

Toward morning he became restless. "What is it?" Father Norbert asked solicitously.

"There is a notebook," Gabriel answered, "in the top

drawer of my desk in which I have written down all the
graces I have received through Mary's hands. I am afraid
the devil will use it to tempt me to vanity. I want you
to destroy it. Don't let anyone see it."

"All right," the director answered soothingly. "I'll burn
it immediately."

With the coming of day, Gabriel seemed to gain a little
strength. The doctor suggested a poultice for his chest
and throat, and that he be given some brandy, but the
patient was beyond the help of these remedies.

About five o'clock that afternoon Father Norbert was
again alone with the patient and noticed a change come
over his face. He rushed out and rang the community
bell. All the religious hurried to the sickroom. Gabriel
smiled at each one and then turned his eyes to the crucifix.
He was plainly in his death struggle.

They said the prayers for the dying and gave him
Viaticum. Then they prayed the rosary. When the Angelus
rang at six he looked beseechingly at a picture of the
Madonna he held in his hands. At seven o'clock the rector
dismissed the religious for supper.

"Isn't the end yet?" Gabriel murmured. "No matter! I
don't want to cut short my sufferings." He turned again
to his crucifix. "I love You, O my Jesus, I love You."

During the night all hell seemed to loose its fury upon
him. The temptations alternated between the grossest forms
of impurity and the subtlest forms of pride. Over and over
Gabriel would blurt out the terrible thoughts that crowded
his mind, pleading for renewed absolution.

Through the long hours the battle for his soul continued.
"The darkness —" Gabriel whispered, "it is awful. . . ."

Suddenly his eyes seemed filled with horror and fright.

"What are they doing here?" he gasped. "They have no business in here! Get those evil women away from me. . . . O God, help me!"

Father Norbert seized the holy water bottle and sprinkled the bed. The seductive phantasms withdrew.

Then came the feeling of conceit. Yes, he had triumphed. Never once had he surrendered his baptismal innocence. It was due wholly to his iron will! "Oh, Father," he cried, "I am so proud. Give me absolution for all my sins of conceit!"

Back and forth the battle raged. Five times that night Father Norbert gave him absolution. "It seemed to be the only thing that would calm him," the priest said later.

As dawn began to streak the eastern sky, Gabriel's features relaxed and a look of peace flooded his countenance.

"Is your conscience perfectly at peace?" Father Norbert whispered.

Gabriel smiled and tried to nod assent.

Father Norbert got up and walked wearily to the window. Dawn was breaking and in the azure sky he could see tiny puffs of cloud turning from pink to white. Tiredly he watched them with tears in his eyes. The whole world was hushed and heaven seemed waiting.

The bell for Prime rang at six o'clock and religious began scurrying down to chapel. Gabriel started searching the covers, pushing his hand around in the blankets.

"Do you want to change position?" Father Norbert asked.

"No . . . I'm looking for the picture of the Madonna."

Father Norbert handed him his picture of the Sorrowful Mother which had slipped down under his habit. It was the picture he had kept before him on his desk; the one he had practically worn away with kisses. He recognized it with joy, kissed it again, and placed it upon his heart. *"Mama mia, spicciati!"* If only his heavenly Mother would hurry!

Gabriel's breathing became more labored. The death rattle sounded in his throat, a raspy sort of sound like heavy cloth torn slowly. Father Norbert went out and rang the community bell. The religious had just begun the Hour of Prime, but they all stopped and came to the sickroom, each bearing a lighted candle. Kneeling about the bed they began the prayers for the dying.

Father Norbert offered Gabriel the crucifix to kiss. Then he repeated the aspirations for a happy death. Gabriel tried falteringly to follow: "Jesus, Joseph, and Mary, I give you my heart and my soul. . . ."

His eyes turned slightly to the left and began to shine with an unearthly radiance. He seemed ravished by some heavenly vision. The religious held their breath. His hands clutched tighter on the picture of the Madonna and his voice grew thin.

"Gesu, Giuseppe, e Maria . . ."

A soft sigh slipped through his lips and the light in his eyes went out. Somewhere down the corridor a clock struck. It was six-thirty on the morning of Thursday, February 27, 1862.

CONCLUSION

Ordinarily a person's face loses all expression at the moment of death. But in the case of Confrater Gabriel it seemed that his countenance assumed the aspect of an ecstasy.

During his illness his cheeks had become sunken, his features clay-colored. The medicines which the doctor had administered to check the tubercle bacilli had given a brownish hue to his skin. But at death all trace of that immediately disappeared and his skin resumed its whiteness. His features became soft and lifelike, giving him the appearance of a youth who had just fallen asleep.

Father Norbert rose from his knees and cast a long, lingering look at the dead student. Then in a voice choked with emotion, he exclaimed, "A great Passionist has gone home to God!" Abruptly he turned and left the room.

It was already the second half of the hour of morning prayer, so the religious returned to the chapel. Father Simon celebrated a Requiem Mass and the community recited the Office of the Dead. Meanwhile, Brothers Sylvester and Charles revested the body in the holy habit and folded the hands over the profession crucifix. Then they arranged it on a wooden slab and carried it to the church, where it was placed on a catafalque before the high altar.

Word of Gabriel's death spread quickly through the little

town of Isola and the surrounding countryside. Throughout the day and night villagers and mountaineers came to
pay their respects and touch religious articles to the body.
At the funeral next morning it seemed that the whole town
was present.

After the obsequies, the church was emptied and the
stone on the floor at the epistle side of the church, which
covered the entrance to the burial crypt, was opened. The
body was slid down into the charnel house and arranged
between the corpses of Confrater Peter and Father Jerome.
The place was then sealed.

A month later Father Norbert wrote a long letter to
Sante Possenti, attempting to comfort him on the loss of
his son.

"Dear Signor Possenti," he began. " 'May the most holy,
adorable, and loving will of God be always accomplished
in and around us.' That was a frequent expression on the
lips of Confrater Gabriel, and may we ourselves repeat it
now with complete resignation. God has given us a son
and He has taken him away. May He be blessed in all that
He does. . . .

"Would you believe it? Owing to my grief and sorrow
I have been bedridden for a whole month. The death of
your son made me so disconsolate that there were some
days when they thought I would follow him. You may think
this an exaggeration, but . . . if you could only see my
heart, you would know. . . .

"The holy life that Confrater Gabriel led and his truly
enviable death makes us morally certain that he is praying
for us who are still in exile. . . . His example has aroused
an emulation in the other students and blessed will they
be, if they imitate him.

"One of our missionaries, who has spent over forty years in the religious life, has made use of Gabriel's beautiful death in preaching to the people. He has found it a means of animating them to sanctity.

"All are praising his virtue and expressing their admiration for him. Many are asking for some object that he used. Some of the people of Isola took strands of his hair, when he was laid out in the church. They use these mementos as relics and say they have received many favors through him. I must admit that I myself have asked many things of him and have received help every time.

"Let us try, therefore, to imitate him. He made such great strides in so few years. In comparison what have we accomplished these many years? To our confusion we must admit that he far surpassed us and reached the fullness of a long career in a very brief time."

That last line of Father Norbert's letter sums up the life and personality of Gabriel Francis Possenti. In five years he became a saint — not by doing extraordinary things, but simply by doing the ordinary ones extraordinarily well!

The fame of his virtues, despite the fact that the Passionists were banished from the monastery in the political turmoil just a year after his death, continued to spread. The little Church of the Immaculate Conception fell into disrepair, but people continued to pray at the spot that marked his grave. Hundreds of miracles were reported.

In 1891 an official investigation into the life and virtues of Confrater Gabriel was opened by the ecclesiastical authorities at Terni, Sante Possenti's birthplace. Then they passed to Assisi, Spoleto, Penne, and Rome. In each place all possible witnesses were summoned before the examiners.

Only thirty years had elapsed since his death, so it was possible to question his immediate family, his three surviving brothers and sister, his former college companions, his teachers, his brothers in religion, his confessors and spiritual directors.

When all the data had been assembled, it was presented to the Sacred Congregation of Rites for judgment. Gaetano Cardinal Alosi-Masella, Prefect of the Congregation, personally took charge of the cause and saw it through the various tribunals.

Six years later the Holy Father received ninety-nine formal petitions to permit the process of beatification to go forward. Thirty were written by cardinals, thirty-five by archbishops and bishops, and thirty-four by superiors general of religious orders. On July 7, 1896, Pope Leo XIII graciously acceded to these many requests and authorized the formal introduction of the cause.

When it was proved that Gabriel of the Sorrowful Virgin had exercised in a heroic degree the theological and moral virtues, he was solemnly beatified in St. Peter's Basilica on May 31, 1908, by Pope Pius X. Many who had known him familiarly in life were present for this ceremony.

Almost immediately his shrine at Isola Gran Sasso became a place of pilgrimage and hundreds of other miracles were reported. The Sacred Congregation of Rites gave a most exact scrutiny to the various testimonials. After sifting the sworn evidence of over a thousand cases, they determined that two of them were absolutely incontestable. John Baptist Cerro had been cured instantaneously of severe arthritis, and Aloysius Parisi had recovered immediately from a grievous abdominal rupture. There could be no doubt of the genuineness of these miracles by which God was attesting the holiness of this faithful Passionist.

The date for the canonization was tentatively set for May, 1913. But with the political upheaval of that time and the subsequent war, the ceremony had to be deferred until May, 1920. When finally Pope Benedict XV proclaimed Gabriel Francis Possenti among the blessed in heaven and the new patron for youth, there were present for the occasion forty-five cardinals, two hundred and eighty bishops, and sixty-one thousand visitors.

Three who had known Gabriel personally were present for this thrilling event: Michael Possenti, Brother Sylvester, and Maria Pannechetti. The Holy Father gave them a special audience and his concluding words were a question: "Sante Possenti thought that his son had made a mistake in joining the Passionists. . . . But if the grand assessor had lived to see the honor accorded his boy today as a Son of the Passion, what would his judgment have been?"

SOURCES

1. *Lettere di San Gabriele dell'Addolorata* — 31 letters written by Confrater Gabriel to his father, brothers, and friends. Teramo, Casa Editrice Typographica Teramana, 1943.

2. Manuscripts of St. Gabriel, including *Simbolo Mariano, Resolutions, Poems,* and *notebooks* on his studies, preserved at Santuario S. Gabriele dell'Addolorata, Isola del Gran Sasso.

3. *Processus Ordinarius Pinnesis* — All public testimony taken at Penne regarding the life, virtues, and miracles of Confrater Gabriel of the Sorrowful Virgin, as well as the official data on the recognition of his body and absence of formal cult. Romae, 1895, Ex Typis Guerra et Mirri, 707 pp.

4. *Processus Romani Additionalis Informativi* — Testimony of the reputation of Confrater Gabriel of the Sorrowful Virgin, his virtues and miracles. Romae, 1895, Ex Typis Guerra et Mirri, 142 pp.

5. *Processus Albanensis* — Additional testimony on the life and virtues of Confrater Gabriel. Romae, Archivum Generale Congr. SS. Crucis et Passionis, 38 pp.

6. *Processus in Curia Ecclesiastica Spoletanna* — All testimony of family, friends, and acquaintances before the Commission at Spoleto, regarding life and virtues of Gabriel Francis Possenti. Romae, Archivum Generale Congr. SS. Crucis et Passionis, 438 pp.

7. *Processus Apostolica Pinnensis* — Further examination into the life and virtues of Confrater Gabriel of the Sorrowful Virgin. Romae, 1898, Ex Typis Pauli Vespasiani, 287 pp.

8. *Processus Apostolica Aprutina* — Special examination of the miracles and virtues ascribed to the Venerable Servant of God, Gabriel of the Sorrowful Virgin. Romae, Archivum Generale Congr. SS. Crucis et Passionis, 1898, 553 pp.

9. *Processus Orginalis Apostolica Romae* — Investigation of miracles worked through the intercession of the Venerable Servant of God,

Gabriel of the Sorrowful Virgin. Romae, Archivum Generale Congr. SS. Crucis et Passionis, 1905, 310 pp.

10. *Processus Apostolica Pontiscurvi* — Investigation of miracles worked through the intercession of Blessed Gabriel of the Sorrowful Virgin, Romae, 1911, Archivum Gen. Congr. SS. Crucis et Passionis, 265 pp.

11. *Processiculi Suppletivi Apostolica Pontiscurvi* — Further investigation of the miracles ascribed to Blessed Gabriel of the Sorrowful Virgin, Romae, 1917, Archivum Gen. Congr. SS. Crucis et Passionis, 50 pp.

12. *Processus Apostolica Gallipolitana* — Investigation of the miracles ascribed to Blessed Gabriel of the Sorrowful Virgin. Romae, 1918, Archivum Gen. Congr. SS. Crucis et Passionis, 158 pp.

13. *Positio Super Introductione Causae* — Data on the introduction of the Cause of Gabriel Francis Possenti, with objections of the Promoter of the Faith and the responses. Romae, 1895, Ex Typis Guerra et Mirri, 507 pp.

14. *Positio Super Validitate Processum* — Cross-examination of the Promoter of the Faith on the testimony of the Apostolic Processes with responses. Romae, 1898, Ex Typis Guerra et Mirri, 184 pp.

15. *Beatificationis Ven. Gabrielis a V.D.* — Positiones super Virtutibus II, Romae, 1899, Ex Typis Pauli Vespasiani, 568 pp.

16. *Judicia Super Duobus Primis Miraculis* — Medical and Legal Examination of the Miracles by Doctor Alexis Murino. Romae, 1906, Ex Typis Juvenum Opifitium a S. Joseph.

17. *Canonizationis B. Gabrielis a V.D.* — Positiones Omnes, Romae, 1908, Ex Typis Pont. Instituti Pii IX.

18. *Acta Apostolicae Sedis — Acta Canonizationum* — Decree of Pope Benedict XV by which Blessed Gabriel of the Sorrowful Virgin was canonized and his feast extended to the Universal Church, Romae, 1920, Ex Typis Vaticanis.

19. *Vita del Giovane Francesco Possenti* — Recollections of Gabriel Francis Possenti by his contemporary, Paul Bonaccia, Torino, 1868, Ex Typis Pietro di G. Marietti.

20. *Vita del Gabriele dell'Addolorata* a Norberto di S. Maria, manuscript account of life of Confrater Gabriel of the Sorrowful Virgin written by his director and found in the provincial archives, Maria SS. della Pieta, Recanati, 1958.

BIBLIOGRAPHY

1. *Vita del Giovane Francesco Possenti,* Paolo Bonaccia, Torino, Marietti, 1868, 266 pp.
2. *Vita del Gabriele Possenti,* Anchiso Chiavatti, Modena, 1893.
3. *Un Esempio ai Giovani, Venerabile Gabrielle dell'Addolorata,* Canon Giovanni Biastiotti, Roma, Desclee, 1898.
4. *The Life of Venerable Gabriel of Our Lady of Sorrows,* Hyacinth Hage, C.P., Philadelphia, Kilner, 1899, 275 pp.
5. *Vie de Saint Gabriel de la Vierge des Dorleures,* P. Bernard, C.P., Paris, Desclee, 1903, 102 pp.
6. *Life of Blessed Gabriel of Our Lady of Sorrows,* Nicholas Ward, C.P., Philadelphia, Kilner, 1910, 295 pp.
7. *Vita di S. Gabriele dell'Addolorata, Studente Passionista,* P. Germano di S. Stanislao, C.P., Roma, Vaticana, 1920, 416 pp.
8. *St. Gabriel of Our Lady of Sorrows,* Reginald Lummer, C.P., Paulist Press, New York, 1920, 32 pp.
9. *Memorias Historicas de Heroico Juvem S. Gabriel,* P. Lorenzo del Cuore di Gesu, Sao Paulo, Discone, 1921.
10. *Vida de San Gabriel de La Virgen Dolorosa,* P. Anselmo de la Dolorosa, C.P., Bilbao, Deusto, 1921, 400 pp.
11. *Saint Gabriel, Passionist,* Fr. Camillus, C.P., Kenedy, New York, 1923, 320 pp.
12. *San Gabriele dell'Addolorata, Chicerco Passionista,* Mons. Stanislao Battistelli, C.P., Societa San Paolo, Roma, 1925, 240 pp.
13. *San Gabrielle dell'Addolorata,* Mons. Pietro Gorla, Casa Edetrice S. Lega Eucharistica, Milan, 1928, 480 pp.
14. *S. Gabriele dell'Addolorata,* P. Stanislaus, C.P., Compatrono della Gioventu Cattolica Italiana, Teramo, 1929, 128 pp.
15. *S. Gabriele dell'Addolorata,* P. Amadeo, C.P., Palatina, Turin, 1930, 64 pp.
16. *Saint Gabriel, Passioniste,* Bernard Latzarus, Mignard, Paris, 1933, 158 pp.
17. *Saint Gabriel de l'Addolorata,* J. Perrin, O.P., Editiones de Cerf, Juviosy, 1936, 95 pp.
18. *Mary's Cavalier,* Osmund Thorp, C.P., Pelligrini, Sidney, Australia, 1937, 24 pp.

19. *Omaggio a San Gabriele dell'Addolorata,* nel lo Centenario della Nascita, 1838–1938, Curia Provincializia dei PP. Passionisti, Recanati, 1938, 190 pp.
20. *That Boy! A Story of Saint Gabriel, C.P.,* Brother Ernest, C.S.C., Dujarie Press, Notre Dame, Ind., 1940, 134 pp.
21. *S. Gabriele dell'Addolorata,* Gilla Gremigni, Florence, 1941.
22. *San Gabriele dell'Addolorata,* P. Elias, C.P., Societas de San Pablo, Madrid, 1942, 197 pp.
23. *La Gloria di S. Gabriel dell'Addolorata,* P. Faustus del Cuore di Maria, C.P., Santuario di S. Gabriele, Teramo, 1942, 90 pp.
24. *S. Gabriel de Nossa Senhora des Dores, Estudiante Passionista,* Padres Passionistas, Barrosilas, Minho, 1943, 276 pp.
25. *Il Serafino dell'Abruzzo,* Don Eugenio Pilla, Turin, 1943.
26. *Saint Gabriel, Passionist Student,* Aloysius McDonough, C.P., Sign Press, Union City, N. J., 1943, 64 pp.
27. *Sao Gabriel de Nossa Senhora des Dores,* P. Silvio, C.P., Redacao de "O Calvario," Sao Paulo, 1944, 247 pp.
28. *S. Gabriel, Passioniste,* P. Hilarion, C.P., Drukkery Missiehus, Sittard, 1946, 220 pp.
29. *Il Devote di S. Gabriele dell'Addolorata,* P. Ilario, C.P., Santuario di S. Gabriel, Teramo, 1946, 339 pp.
30. *Storia del Santuario di San Gabriele dell'Addolorata,* P. Ilario, C.P., Santuario di S. Gabriel, Teramo, 1947, 63 pp.
31. *Il Santa del Gran Sasso,* P. Ilario, C.P., Santuario di S. Gabriele, Teramo, 1949, 200 pp.
32. *Saint Gabriel,* Mabel Farnum, Society of St. Paul, Youngstown, Ohio, 1950, 235 pp.
33. *Der Gepfelstummer,* Deutschen Passionisten, Obensberg, 1952, 52 pp.
34. *Saint Gabriel of Our Lady of Sorrows,* Joseph Smith, C.P., Catholic Truth Society of Ireland, Dublin, 1955, 24 pp.
35. *La Vita Contemplativa in S. Gabriele dell'Addolorata,* P. Casimiro Lorenzetti, C.P., Santuario di S. Gabriele, Teramo, 1955, 64 pp.
36. *San Gabriele dell'Addolorata,* P. Casimiro Lorenzetti, C.P., Santuario di S. Gabriele, Teramo, 1956, 71 pp.
37. *Recorrenza Centenaria,* per il primo centenario della Prov. di Maria SS. della Pieta, Recanati, 1951.
38. *L'Eco di San Gabriele,* Bolletino Settemale de Santuario di San Gabriele, Teramo, No. 1–20.
39. *Il Maestro e Il Discepolo,* P. Natale Cavatassi, C.P., Sanctuario di S. Gabriele, Teramo, 1958, 53 pp.
40. *Happy Was My Youth,* Edmund Burke, C.P., M. H. Gill and Son, Ltd. Dublin Ireland, 1961, 262 pp.